AS

CriticalThinking
for OCR

Jacquie Thwaites

www.heinemann.co.uk
✓ Free online support
✓ Useful weblinks
✓ 24 hour online ordering

01865 888058

Heinemann
Inspiring generations

Heinemann Educational Publishers
Halley Court, Jordan Hill, Oxford OX2 8EJ
Part of Harcourt Education

Heinemann is a registered trademark of
Harcourt Education Limited

© Jacquie Thwaites, 2005

First published 2005

10 09 08 07 06 05
10 9 8 7 6 5 4 3 2 1

British Library Cataloguing in Publication Data is available
from the British Library on request.

10-digit ISBN: 0435 23581 8
13-digit ISBN: 978 0 435235 81 9

Designed by Lorraine Inglis
Typeset by Techset

Printed in the UK by Bath Press Ltd

Cover photo: M.C. Escher's 'Symmetry Drawing E57' © 2005
The M.C. Escher Company Holland.

Acknowledgements
Every effort has been made to contact copyright holders of material
reproduced in this book, and to ensure that information is correct at the
time of printing. However, the publisher will be pleased to rectify any
omissions in subsequent printings if notice is given.

Extract and picture re: The Big Bang Theory, taken from
www.nasa.gov © NASA. Extract and photograph re: Jamie Oliver, from
Daily Express Saturday Magazine, 9th March 2005. © Express Newspapers.
Reprinted with permission. Article 'Royal marriage can go ahead; says
registrar' by Sally Pook, The Daily Telegraph, 10th March 2005.
© Telegraph Group Limited 2005. Reprinted with permission.

Contents

Introduction to Critical Thinking

What is Critical Thinking?

Critical Thinking is a skills-based subject that assesses and develops arguments. It involves three central skills that you use in your everyday lives:

- Understanding what an argument is claiming
- Assessing if the argument works
- Constructing an effective argument of your own.

These three basic skills can be developed through practising the more advanced skills of logical reasoning:

- **ANALYSIS** of argument
- **EVALUATION** of argument
- **DEVELOPMENT** of argument.

Why study Critical Thinking?

Critical Thinking gives you transferable skills that will help you to approach tasks in all your other subjects with more confidence. The list below shows some of the strategies you will develop.

- *Identifying the precise focus of an argument* – this may be in an article, report, advert, documentary or interview.
- *Evaluating the reasoning* given to support the overall claim. In the past you may have felt that there was a weakness in an argument but have been unable to put it into words. Critical Thinking can give you the terminology and skills to identify both strengths and weaknesses in reasoning.
- *Evaluating evidence* – Critical Thinking can help you to evaluate how well a piece of evidence supports a claim.
- *Assessing the credibility of sources* – where there are differing accounts or perspectives about events, Critical Thinking can help you to make judgements about the strengths and weaknesses of the evidence.
- *Producing clear, well structured and powerful arguments.* This is a skill valued both in essays and in coursework, where you are often required to test out a hypothesis, present evidence and reach a conclusion. It is also useful in essays where you are required to make a reasoned case in response to a question.

These strategies can be used to increase your understanding and powers of evaluation and persuasion in many areas of day-to-day life. You can apply them in the workplace, as a consumer and in relationships – in fact, wherever logical reasoning is required.

The word 'critical' might at first lead you to think that Critical Thinking is a purely negative exercise. However, a critique should enable you to identify both the strengths and weaknesses of arguments and to come to a reasoned judgement.

Now look at the following examples of Critical Thinking in action.

Critical Thinking in action

We live in an age when the media attempts to influence our choices. You may be unconvinced by the evidence, but not be able to say why it is weak. Critical Thinking can help your judgement by directing you to look at common areas of weakness. In the example below, Critical Thinking highlights what important information is *left out*.

JUICIO
Light

The healthy option for children

Contains no added sugars

This advert has failed to mention that the drink has artificial sweeteners such as aspartame, which may also incur health risks. This would weaken the advert's claim that Juicio is the healthy option, since the risks from aspartame may be greater than those from added sugars.

Arguments at school, at home or in the workplace can also be unconvincing, but under pressure it may be difficult to think of a reasoned response.

Imagine that you have waited a long time for some handmade shelving, and you phone the company to complain about the delay. It is a large firm with its own team of carpenters, electricians and painters to deal with all installation and repair work.

At first the manager's response might seem reasonable. However, unless the electricians also carry out carpentry work, or the electrical work requires carpentry, emergency work that has to be carried out by electricians seems to have little relevance to a delay to a carpentry job.

Critical Thinking will give you the reasoning skills to spot such *irrelevance* quickly, and respond appropriately.

You may sometimes be aware that an argument has left out something essential, but you are unsure of what it is. Critical Thinking can help you to develop confidence in identifying the *assumptions*, or necessary missing reasons, so that you can point out what must be supposed to be true for you to accept the claim that is being made. Consider the following advert:

The advert suggests that teaching is a logical decision if you have a degree and like working with children. However, there is an assumption about the graduate's values. The graduate might value a higher salary above their liking of working with children, or value other areas of work more.

If the assumptions in the argument are made explicit, the advice does not sound so attractive. It would read:

> *'Are you a graduate who likes working with children*
> *and who doesn't value a higher salary than that of teaching*
> *and who doesn't have values above liking working with children*
> *and who doesn't want to work with children in other capacities?*
> *Why not ... Teach'*

Practising the skill of finding assumptions will help you to assess possible weaknesses in everyday persuasion more quickly.

You can equally be faced with adverts that appear to be convincing until you consider the *credibility* of the source of the evidence. The fictional advert below recommends a particular action when choosing car insurance.

Desperate to drive your first car?

If you are aged 17–21, you could save hundreds of pounds on your car insurance ...

SaferCars *is an insurance scheme aimed at helping new young drivers. A young driver is often penalised financially even before they sit behind the wheel of their first car.* **SaferCars** *is the Number One provider of car insurance for 17–21-year-olds and is also recognised as offering the best value for money*. So why not call us today?*

*Source: *SaferCars* Newsletter, August 2005

You might want to question how believable this claim is, that is, its credibility. First, the purpose of the advertisement is to sell you car insurance, so the company has a motive to show their product in the best light. Second, their claims to be the market leader and best value come from a publication they produce themselves. Critical Thinking will help you to be more aware of the strengths and weaknesses of claims such as these.

OCR AS Critical Thinking

The OCR AS Level in Critical Thinking asks you to apply your skills in logical reasoning to evidence and arguments taken from a wide variety of contexts and sources.

The examination is modular. There are two units at AS Level that can be taken in the January and/or May examination sessions:

Unit 1   Credibility of Evidence: a written examination of 1 hr 15 mins

Unit 2   Assessing and Developing Argument: a written examination of 1 hr 45 mins.

There is no coursework – the subject is assessed by examination only.

What does the examination assess?

The three Assessment Objectives are the criteria against which your answers will be marked in each unit. They coincide with the three skills identified as being central to the study of Critical Thinking.

AO 1   **Analysis** of argument
'Analyse critically the use of different kinds of reasoning in a wide range of contexts.'

AO 2   **Evaluation** of argument
'Evaluate critically the use of different kinds of reasoning in a wide range of contexts.'

AO 3   **Development** of argument
'Develop and communicate relevant and coherent arguments clearly and accurately in a concise and logical manner.'

Unit 1 represents 40% of the AS level, 20% of the A Level
Unit 2 represents 60% of the AS level, 30% of the A Level

You can use the AS Level to progress to an Advanced Level (A2) in Critical Thinking. This also has two units:

Unit 3 Resolution of dilemmas
Unit 4 Critical reasoning.

You can find full details in the OCR specification, available at www.ocr.org.uk. There are Heinemann textbooks covering Units 2, 3 and 4.

What is credibility of evidence?

When you talk about the **credibility** of evidence, you are asking the question: 'How believable is this evidence?' You are not at this point looking for weaknesses in reasoning. Nor are you deciding whether or not something is true. There is a difference between credibility and trust. This book will show you how to assess sources and make a judgement about a dispute. However this will not enable you to decide the truth of the matter only how likely it is that something is the case.

Unit 1 of your exam requires you:

- **to assess the credibility of evidence**
- **to make a reasoned judgement** using the insights gained from your assessment.

You will be asked to assess the credibility of **personal evidence**, visual evidence and documents. This will help you to make a judgement in areas where there is some doubt.

In some situations there is little doubt about what happened because there is considerable evidence in the form of documents, or visual and other material. In these cases the personal evidence, for example the claims that are made by witnesses, is more easily assessed as being believable or not against this evidence.

> *The M25 around London is a congested route at peak times. Motorway cameras provide video footage, and daily radio travel reports confirm this. There would be little reason therefore to doubt anyone who claimed that their journey to work along the M25 had been delayed by traffic problems. Their claim could be taken as credible, unless there were strong reasons relating to this case to disbelieve them. A motorway video shot of their car in a stream of slowly moving traffic could be taken as **conclusive evidence** of their claim.*

KEY TERMS

Credibility – whether the evidence is believable

Personal evidence – a claim made by a witness or other contributor

Conclusive evidence – evidence that leaves little room for doubt

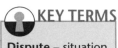

KEY TERMS

Dispute – situation where the evidence is inconclusive, that is, incomplete, unclear or open to interpretation

In other situations there is a **dispute** about what happened because the evidence is inconclusive. Here you are faced with conflicting reports; you need to assess which evidence is more credible, so that you can reach a judgement about what happened, or who was to blame.

In traffic accidents there is often a balance of evidence on both sides, so that it is difficult to judge who is to blame. The opposing claims may be 'He did not give way at the junction' and 'She was speeding around the roundabout'. Faced with the difficult decision about which evidence to believe, you will need a strategy to help you to assess the credibility of the conflicting evidence.

How will this book help me to assess credibility of evidence?

Chapter 1: Understanding the key criteria

This chapter will explain how you can assess the credibility of evidence by asking:

- What motive would this person have to misrepresent the truth?
- How likely is it that they could have perceived or interpreted the events correctly?
- What are the strengths and weaknesses of the evidence given?

While you work through this book you will look at a range of disputes concerning legal, medical, sporting and military matters, among others.

There will also be activities to give you the opportunity to apply these criteria.

Was the referee right to award a free kick?

Please note, the identity of the individual in the photograph has been protected.

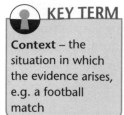

Chapter 2: Applying the key criteria

This will explain how to apply these criteria to the:

- **context** of the dispute
- documents in which the evidence is presented
- images used to support the claims
- personal evidence given in the dispute.

As these are the four areas assessed in the examination there will also be exam tips to help you to focus your answers, sample answers to help you to identify the skills required and sample questions to help you to test out your skills.

Chapter 3: Producing a reasoned judgement

This chapter will explain how you can reach a reasoned judgement by asking:

- Which claims agree and which conflict?
- Who is on whose side?
- Does the evidence of one side outweigh that of the other?
- Is the evidence of one side more credible than the other?

You will also find exam tips, sample questions and sample answers.

Chapter 4: Exam practice

This chapter will explain what the question paper will ask you to do and what it will be looking for in your answers. Additionally it will suggest how you can prepare for the exam.

Chapter 5: Guidance to the activities

This chapter provides sample answers for the activities in Chapters 1 to 4, along with general advice on tackling similar questions.

Understanding the key criteria

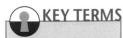

KEY TERMS

Credibility criteria – tools to help you assesss whether a claim is believable

Motive – reason to lie or to tell the truth

KEY TERMS

Perception – obtaining information by using the senses

Visual evidence – any evidence of a non-textual nature, such as photographs, maps, tables and line

Documentary evidence – any evidence of a textual nature, such as newspaper articles and websites

EXAM TIP

*Focus on using these ten **credibility criteria**. Applying these represents a large proportion of the marks on the exam paper.*

This chapter will show you how to apply **credibility criteria**. These are the tools that allow you to assess whether a claim is credible (believable).

There are ten key credibility criteria. The first five relate to the **motives** someone may have to tell the truth or to lie:

1 Neutrality
2 Bias
3 Vested interest to lie
4 Vested interest to tell the truth
5 Reputation

Applying these criteria will help you to answer the question:

> *How likely is it that this person is telling the truth?*

The next two criteria relate to **perception**:

6 Ability to observe
7 Relevant expertise

Applying these criteria will help you to answer the question:

> *How likely is it that this person could interpret events correctly?*

The final three criteria will help you to assess the strength or weakness of **visual evidence** and **documentary evidence** in Unit 1, although they will have a wider application to reasoning in Units 2, 3 and 4.

8 Relevance
9 Significance
10 Selectivity

Applying these criteria to evidence of any kind will help you to answer the question:

> *How well does this evidence support the claim?*

Motive

How likely is it that this person is telling the truth?

To answer this question you will need to examine possible motives, that is, reasons to lie or to tell the truth. However, you should always bear in mind that the possibility of a motive does not guarantee that this has actually prompted the response.

> *Someone who is late for work has a motive to lie to cover up any shortcomings, such as sleeping through their alarm. They might say they have been delayed by heavy traffic. However, just because the circumstances indicate a motive to lie, you cannot be certain that the person is not telling the truth – they may indeed have been caught in heavy traffic.*

Neutrality

CREDIBILITY CRITERION 1

KEY TERMS

Source – where the evidence comes from; it could be a person, as here, or a document

Neutral – having no motive to lie

If a **source** is said to be **neutral**, it means that they have no known motive to lie or to distort what is being reported. Bystanders, religious leaders, the police, judges and referees *might* be expected to be neutral.

- Bystanders *might* simply have no involvement in the situation to prompt any distortion.

> *A bystander on the edge of a public disturbance, where rival football supporters are exchanging insults and physical violence, might be expected to give an unbiased account of what happened, because they are not involved in the situation and have nothing to gain from lying or taking sides, if they do not know any of the participants.*

- Some people *might* have such strong beliefs about the importance of truth that you would expect them always to tell the truth. People with religious convictions, such as priests and imams, might be expected to tell the truth in accordance with their beliefs in the value of the truth.

- An impartial assessment *might* be expected from other people by nature of their profession. Judges, the police and referees are expected to make professional judgements that look at evidence openly without prejudice or bias. In fact, it is in their interest to be seen to be unbiased and honest; acting otherwise might risk their professional reputation and ultimately their job.

> *If a policeman were present at the disturbance described above, you might expect him/her still to give truthful evidence against supporters even if he was a member of the same football club as them.*

> *An OfSTED Inspector might be expected not to distort the results of a school inspection when grading teaching and learning. Their professionalism should ensure their neutrality.*

Factors that might reduce someone's neutrality

You probably noticed that the word '*might*' was used above with each expectation of neutrality. In all three examples there could be circumstances that might prompt the person to tell a lie or distort the truth. To assess their credibility fully you need to discount anything in the circumstances that might lead to biased evidence.

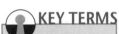

KEY TERMS

Suppositional reasoning – supposing something to be true to draw a conclusion; also known as **hypothetical reasoning**

Assumption – what must be supposed to be the case to draw your conclusion

> *The bystander on the edge of the disturbance between football supporters might be a supporter of one of the clubs. Alternatively, he might know the people he should report as being violent and be afraid of the consequences for himself. In either case, he might be selective in what he reported, or might lie to protect himself.*

If you were to claim, '*The bystander would have no reason to lie*' you would need to add the conditions '*if he did not support either of the football clubs and did not know the people concerned*'.

Here you have used **suppositional reasoning**. Where the evidence does not give you the full picture, you need to identify what additional conditions must be true in order for you to make this assessment. In this way you are making clear your **assumptions**, that is, what must be supposed to be the case to draw your conclusion.

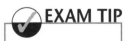

EXAM TIP

You will be asked to 'identify any factors which you must suppose to be true' when you assess personal evidence – this means using suppositional reasoning.

This is also known as **hypothetical reasoning** and takes the form: 'If ... then ...' or 'Unless ... then ...' The words *might, if, probably, provided, supposing, assuming* are used to take account of the missing information. Suppositional reasoning is an important part of assessing personal evidence. Activity 1 will give you practice in using this skill.

ACTIVITY

Work in a group. You might expect the following sources, under normal circumstances, to be unbiased. Think of as many reasons as you can why each of the sources might not be neutral when making claims.

Express your reasons for each source in the format:

_____ *might be expected to be neutral because …*

but this neutrality would be weakened if …

A *A religious leader*

B *A competition judge*

C *A football referee*

D *A health and safety inspector*

E *A news reader*

Please note, the identities of the individuals in the photographs have been protected.

Bias

CREDIBILITY CRITERION 2

KEY TERM

Bias – a motive or subconscious reason to lie or distort the truth in order to protect or blame someone else or to support strongly held beliefs

Bias is the opposite of neutrality, in that the source has a motive or subconscious reason to lie or to distort the truth by being selective or incomplete in what they report. Their motive, however, is not for personal gain but the effect that the lie has on another person.

- **Bias could reflect a motive to support someone** close, such as a family member, friend, colleague or team member.

> *In a car accident, the passenger may lie about the speed at which they were travelling to protect the friend who was giving them a lift.*

- **Bias could reflect a motive to blame someone** against whom the person is prejudiced.

> *In a car accident, a bystander may lie about who caused the crash, because they were envious of his expensive sports car.*

- It could be argued that there is always an element of **natural bias**, in that we all have a perspective which influences our claims.

> *On the morning of 5 April 2003, when the Americans took Baghdad, there were two conflicting claims. The Iraqi Minister of Information claimed that the Americans had not entered the city, whilst the Americans claimed that they were in the heart of Baghdad.*
>
> *There was little dispute about the position of the American troops, but for Americans used to large cities, being in the outskirts indicated being in the city. However, for the Iraqis the centre of the city meant the central square. In each case what they claimed was possibly determined by their cultural bias and their understanding of 'city'. However, there might also have been a measure of vested interest (see next page) to distort the truth to boost morale, which would also motivate the difference in their claims.*

CREDIBILITY CRITERION 3

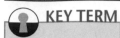

KEY TERM

Vested interest – a motive to lie or to tell the truth because the person has something to gain or to avoid losing

Vested interest to lie

Someone with a **vested interest** has a motive, which may be subconscious, to lie or to tell the truth because they will benefit in some way from the outcome.

- Here the motive to lie has an outcome from which **the source will possibly benefit**.

> *The driver involved in a car accident would have a vested interest to lie if guilty of speeding, to avoid an insurance claim against them or prosecution for dangerous driving. This would weaken the credibility of their evidence.*
>
> *In a disputed basketball foul, the team captain and manager would have a vested interest to lie to try to persuade the referee that their team member was innocent, to avoid penalties or the team member being sent off.*

- Vested interest can also be identified in documentary evidence, which can be selective or over/underplayed in such a way that it promotes the interest of those presenting the report.

> *The results of research into the effects of vitamins upon general health may misrepresent the truth if they are published by a business such as a health food manufacturer that would benefit financially from a positive interpretation of the research.*

CREDIBILITY CRITERION 4

Vested interest to tell the truth

There are a number of reasons why someone may have a **vested interest to tell the truth**.

- Any witness in a court of law has a vested interest to tell the truth because if they are caught out in a lie they can be tried for (or charged with) perjury, which is a serious and punishable offence.

- Many people have a vested interest to tell the truth because it is required of them professionally – to tell a lie would endanger their professional reputation.

A police constable would have a vested interest to tell the truth when reporting the car accident above, as a lie or a selective report might jeopardise their job.

The referee of the basketball match would have a vested interest not to be swayed by the claims made by the opposing teams, but to follow his professional judgement, as otherwise he would lose public confidence.

ACTIVITY 2

 REMEMBER

Bias is a motive or subconscious reason to lie or distort the truth in order to protect or blame someone else or to support strongly held beliefs.

Vested interest reflects personal gain or loss.

In the scenario below identify which sources could be said to be biased and which to have a vested interest. Justify your decisions by giving reasons.

A case of shoplifting or of forgetfulness?

While Laura was out shopping during the January sales for an outfit to wear at a club night out, she was accused of shoplifting. The store detective said, 'I watched her deliberately hide a pair of shoes in her bag and saw that she didn't present them at the check out.'

Laura claimed, 'It was an honest mistake.' She added that she had chosen the shoes that she wanted to buy and had put the shoes in her bag so that she could have both hands free while she was choosing a top. She explained that by the time she got to the check out, she had forgotten that the shoes were in her bag. She said that she felt very embarrassed about the whole incident and wanted to pay for the shoes.

Laura's neighbour Amira, a shop assistant in the store, said, 'For the last couple of years the store has been short of self-service baskets during the January sales. Customers have often been forced to find other ways to carry multiple purchases.'

CREDIBILITY CRITERION 5

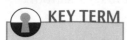

KEY TERM

Reputation – when knowledge of past performance or of character is used to strengthen or weaken the credibility of present claims

Reputation

When people talk about a source's *credentials*, they mean their credence or reliability – their **reputation**. This can work both ways, in that it can weaken or strengthen the credibility of evidence.

- An organisation may have strong credentials because they have a reputation for providing accurate data that can be relied upon.

> *Census data is widely used because the Office for National Statistics has a reputation for supplying reliable material that can underpin research.*

- Evidence also gains credibility if it comes from an individual who has a reputation for honesty and lack of self-interest.

> *Mother Teresa had a reputation for selflessness which made her appeals for help credible, because people thought she was unlikely to be motivated by self-enrichment.*

- In contrast, a reputation for distorting evidence or a past history of negative performance might make a source's evidence less believable.

> *Many people are wary of the publication of school league tables because there are many different versions, depending on which criteria are used. A school can come third nationally according to one version, but not figure in the top twenty according to another. Such a reputation for variation might weaken credibility.*
>
> *A claim made by a politician with a reputation for breaking promises might also be seen as having weak credibility.*

However a *past* reputation, whether positive or negative, cannot be taken as a definite indication that a person or organisation would have acted in a similar way on this *present* occasion. This is where suppositional reasoning is useful. An assessment of credibility could claim, '**If** the source's reputation is a reliable guide to present action then …'.

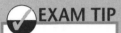
ACTIVITY 3

✔ EXAM TIP

You will probably be asked to assess real documents on the exam paper.

Working in groups, examine a variety of newspaper articles. List the claims that are based on an appreciation of reputation, whether positive or negative.

! REMEMBER

Reputation might weaken or strengthen credibility based on past experience, but this may not relate to the present situation.

Perception

! REMEMBER

Two key criteria relate to perception – ability to observe and relevant expertise.

How likely is this person to know what really happened?

The ability to report an event correctly is influenced by how far it has been perceived correctly. To answer the question above, you need to look at two key criteria:

- How much could the person actually observe of the event?
- What relevant expertise did the person have to help them interpret the situation correctly?

However, before looking at these criteria, you need to be able to distinguish between different types of evidence. This will help you to answer the question:

- Did this person actually observe the event?

Types of evidence

First you need to decide whether a source is giving **eye-witness** evidence, **hearsay evidence** or a **character reference**. Each of these types of claim can offer evidence, but they have different strengths and weaknesses in terms of credibility/believability.

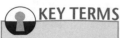

KEY TERMS

Eye witness – someone who provides evidence based on first-hand experience

Hearsay evidence – evidence based on second-hand information from another source, who may have interpreted it

Character reference – evidence given about the character or reputation of one of the sources involved, which doesn't relate to the event itself

- **Eye-witness** accounts are normally seen as a stronger source of evidence than second-hand accounts because they are based on first-hand, direct experience of the event. However, evidence given by those who were present still has to be evaluated against other criteria, such as distance and obstructions.

> *In the car accident referred to on page 10, the driver on the roundabout was accused of speeding and the other driver was accused of pulling out without stopping and giving way. The evidence of both drivers and the passenger would be classed as eye-witness accounts or primary information as they were actually present at the accident.*

- **Hearsay evidence** is information presented about the event by a source who has received the information second-hand, from someone else.

> *According to a paramedic attending the accident, a bystander told him that the car pulling out almost knocked them down as they were crossing the road and then did not stop to give way at the roundabout. The paramedic's evidence would be regarded as hearsay evidence.*

Hearsay evidence would normally be seen as weaker than an eye-witness account because it depends upon two levels of interpretation:
- the perception of the eye witness
- the interpretation given to their evidence by the person who reports it. They might have altered the meaning of what was said for one of several reasons. The evidence may have been misheard; or it may have been selectively reported, missing out certain information, or embellished with extra detail, exaggerated or understated.

If the paramedic's attention was focused on dealing with the injured, she may have misheard what the bystander was saying. The claim might actually have been that the car did not stop and give way to the bystanders as they were crossing the road rather than that it did not stop at the roundabout.

- Evidence given that does not directly comment on this event, but refers to a source's reputation or character in relation to whatever is being assessed, would be classed as a **character reference** given by a character witness.

The employer of the car driver accused of pulling out without stopping might later have given a character reference, for example, 'He is a very careful driver and hasn't been involved in any incidents while working for our firm.'

Because the character witness only refers to reputation, their evidence has less force than claims about this event. Their information about the past does not guarantee that the source would have acted in any particular way in this present incident.

ACTIVITY ❹

In this activity you are going to work in a group to differentiate between eye-witness or primary evidence, hearsay evidence and character reference.

a) Take a piece of A3 paper and divide it into three columns headed *Primary evidence*, *Hearsay evidence* and *Character reference*.

Primary evidence	Hearsay evidence	Character reference

b) Now look back at the scenario in Activity 2: A case of shoplifting or of forgetfulness? Identify a claim that is primary evidence and put this in the first column.

c) Now develop the scenario by adding new sources in columns 2 and 3. Add:
- a claim that is hearsay evidence
- a claim that is a character reference.

CREDIBILITY CRITERION 6

KEY TERM

Ability to observe – the ability of a source to use any of their senses to assess the event

Ability to observe

This criterion helps you to answer the question:

How well could this person observe the event?

When you assess the credibility of eye-witness evidence it is important to assess the degree to which the source was able to observe the event. This could involve any of the senses: sight, hearing, smell, touch or taste.

These are some of the key questions to ask about the source:

- How much of the incident did they see? For example, were they there from the start of the incident (the *outset*)?
- Was their sight restricted, for example by obstructions, their distance from the event, the angle at which they were standing or poor visibility due to weather conditions?
- Were they concentrating on the event or was there anything that might have distracted their attention?
- Did they have any problems with their eyesight?

Many of the above restrictions would also apply to hearing:

- Was their hearing restricted by obstructions, distance, angle, distracting noise or hearing impairment?

When assessing credibility of evidence you could express such assessments as follows:

- In a football match a referee's claim that a player had been fouled, may be weakened if the referee was at a distance from the event or if other payers were obstructing his line of vision.

ACTIVITY 5

Work in a group to identify restrictions to observation. Outline a scenario, and give the claims of one or more sources where there is restricted vision and one or more where there is restricted hearing. Now use this restriction to show how this might weaken the credibility of the claim using the example above to guide you.

Choose from one of the scenarios on page 21 or think of your own:

REMEMBER

When assessing **observation** think about:

- Obstructions
- Distance
- Angle
- Visibility
- Distraction
- Personal ability
- Outset.

Ability to observe includes hearing as well as seeing. In fact, it can involve any of the five senses.

- a disputed football foul
- the theft of a mobile phone at a pop concert
- a pile up on a motorway.

You could start in one of these ways:

- 'The first thing that I saw was ...' (The first thing seen may not have been the start of the event)
- 'The official who was the nearest to the ...' (The nearest person may have been some distance away).

CREDIBILITY CRITERION 7

KEY TERM

Relevant expertise – the skills, experience or training that would help a person to interpret the situation correctly

Relevant expertise

This criterion answers the question:

> *Does this person have the relevant expertise to interpret the event correctly?*

Correct perception of an event requires not only that the event has been observed correctly but also that the source has the ability to interpret the event correctly.

Relevant expertise might strengthen the credibility of a source because of the particular insight which their expertise gives them. Their skills, experience or training could lead them to make accurate claims.

REMEMBER

To assess the credibility of personal evidence, use the criteria:

- **Motive:**
1 Neutrality
2 Bias
3 Vested interest to lie
4 Vested interest to tell the truth
5 Reputation

- **Perception:**
6 Ability to observe
7 Relevant expertise

> *These people would all be expected to have an insight into the situation that might strengthen the credibility of their claims:*
> - *a Wimbledon linesman calling a foot fault*
> - *a doctor assessing the risk of an epidemic*
> - *a building inspector reporting an infringement of building regulations.*

This expertise would normally be seen to strengthen the credibility of their claims above those of other people, although experts sometimes do misjudge situations and there might be other factors that would reduce the credibility of their claims, such as not seeing the full event.

ACTIVITY 6

In each of the examples below, differentiate between relevant and irrelevant expertise.

a) State the expertise of the source.

b) Identify the expertise required to make the claim.

c) Decide whether the source's expertise is relevant in this case.

d) Justify your decision.

A An advert in which a successful and long-lived athlete recommends a particular food as being a healthy product on the grounds that they have always eaten it.

B Advice by UK weather reporters to avoid any unnecessary journeys because of impending blizzard conditions over the whole of the UK.

C Jamie Oliver's criticism of school dinners.

JAMIE'S SCHOOL DINNERS

This is one of the most thought-provoking TV series in years. Jamie's simple point, after all, is that the disgracefully lazy, irresponsible, cheapskate decision to feed schoolkids a relentless nutrition–free diet of junk will have the most terrifying long-term knock-on effects.

Taken from the Daily Express Saturday Magazine, *9 March 2005*

Applying the criteria

All seven of the criteria you have looked at so far need to be applied collectively to assess the overall credibility of a source, whether it is a document or personal evidence, to build up a balanced picture of strengths and weaknesses. The criteria also need to be applied to assess the credibility of the context (the situation in which the evidence arises). You will be given guidance and practice in applying the credibility criteria to these areas in Chapter 2.

EXAM TIP

*In Unit 1 you may
be asked to assess
the strength that
visual evidence gives
to claims.*

Visual and documentary evidence

You will often find that images may be used to support claims. To help you to assess the strength or weakness of visual and documentary evidence you can use these three additional criteria:

8 Relevance

9 Significance

10 Selectivity

CREDIBILITY CRITERION 8

KEY TERM

Relevance – how
directly the visual or
other evidence
relates to the claims
being made

Relevance

This criterion will help you to answer the question: 'Is this evidence relevant to support the claim that is being made?'

- First identify the claim that the evidence is intended to support.
- Next determine whether the images directly relate to these claims.

Imagine a dispute about whether a pop festival held on the outskirts of a small town caused more trouble than it was worth. The negative claims are that:

- huge numbers of people swamped the countryside
- business was taken away from local traders.

What function would the images below play in such a report?

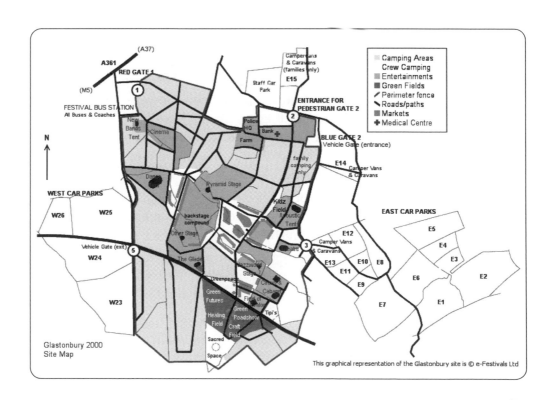

Glastonbury 2000
Site Map

This graphical representation of the Glastonbury site is © e-Festivals Ltd

The claims relate to the effects caused by huge numbers of people and the provision of alternative trading to that in the town. Neither of the images is directly relevant to the claims because they do not illustrate these effects. However, we could look at them for information that might make the claimed effects more credible.

- A scale on the map might have given some indication of the size of the event, or the number of car parking spaces might have indicated the potential capacity of the site. As neither is given, the map is not relevant in deducing the size of the event in relation to the small town. However, even if these had been included, they might not have been a good indication of the numbers of people attending, since the event might have been undersubscribed or oversubscribed, with people coming on foot or parking elsewhere.

- The map does indicate that stalls were present, but not what they were selling or in what quantity. This does not support the claim that the festival took business away from local traders.

- The photograph simply shows certain fans sitting on the ground. This has no relevance to the claim about the effects of large numbers of people or the effect of the festival upon local trade.

This example shows how images used in reports may have no direct relevance to the claims being made, but act merely as an illustration or explanation to help the reader visualise the context, for example the location of the event or the people involved.

ACTIVITY ❼

One great dispute about the beginning of the universe is whether or not it was caused by a Big Bang. What relevance would this image have to the dispute?

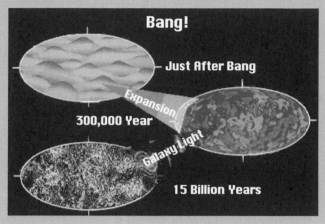

🔑 **KEY TERM**

Significance – the weight of support given by the evidence when seen in the whole context

Significance

If you are presented with images that are directly related to the claim, a further question can be asked: 'What weight does the evidence give to the claim?'

The **significance** of this evidence depends upon how much weight it gives to the claim, when the whole context is taken into consideration.

Suppose that the photograph and caption below were added to the evidence about the pop festival.

Litter was strewn across the countryside

The photograph is *relevant* to the claim about litter; however, its *significance* needs to be determined. To do this you would need to know:

- how much litter would normally be found on this site, to be able to assess the increase in litter that had resulted from the festival
- whether this was distinctive festival litter, for example leaflets, programmes or take-away food debris
- the amount of litter overall, to assess whether this was a small or large proportion of it. If this was a large proportion of the litter, but confined to a small area, then the overall problem might not have been significant.

Without this additional knowledge it would be difficult to work out what weight the photograph gives to the claim. When assessing its significance you could express your answer as:

> *If this countryside was normally clear of litter, or this was distinctive festival litter, or the photo shows only a small proportion of the amount of litter overall, then it would strengthen the negative claims that litter was strewn across the countryside.*

Thus, when determining significance, you should look at the evidence within the context of the whole problem or event.

CREDIBILITY CRITERION 10

Selectivity

 **KEY TERM**

Selectivity – partial evidence e.g. evidence to make a point

Another question can be asked to determine the support that the image gives to the claims:

> *Has the whole context been given or have parts been selectively presented to make a point?*

Where evidence is selective, the whole context may not be apparent and the selection given may not be representative of the whole.

Suppose that the photograph and caption below were added to the evidence about the pop festival being 'more trouble than it was worth'.

Police arresting festival goers. The festival was ruined by fights

The photograph does not depict a fight, but implies that this is the aftermath of a fight. It may be that the writer has selected this photograph to present a negative image of the festival.

To determine whether this was selective evidence, you would need to know:

- whether there were a number of such fights, making this photograph representative of the whole festival experience
- whether this fight was representative of what happened in other areas of the festival or if the fights were limited to one small area not affecting the majority of those present.

In your answer you could assess the support the image provides by stating:

> *This image could give support to the claim in the caption that the festival was ruined by fights, unless one untypical event had been selected to present a negative image. The image would not support the claim either if such fights had been confined to one area, so that the majority of people would not have realised that a disturbance had happened.*

In Activity 8 you can use what you have learned about the effect that relevance, significance and selectivity can have upon the support that images and other evidence can give to claims.

ACTIVITY **8**

 REMEMBER

When an image is given to support a claim, always identify the claim before you identify the support the image gives.

Look at the news story below. Assess what support the photograph gives to the claims that are made.

THE NEEDS OF THE LOCAL COMMUNITY ARE NOT BEING ADDRESSED

The present congested road network is seriously affecting both local business and the quality of life of the people who live and work in the town.

Yet another queue for town centre drivers

Chapter 1 introduced you to ten criteria which you can use to assess the credibility of evidence. Chapter 2 will show you how to apply them so that you can target the marks on the first two parts of the examination paper. Chapter 3 will introduce additional criteria such as corroboration, which will help you to build up a reasoned case which is examined in the final part of the examination paper.

SUMMARY

Credibility: 'how far can we believe this?'
Suppositional reasoning asks what you must suppose to be true to draw this conclusion.

MOTIVE – reason to lie or to tell the truth

1 **Neutrality** – having no motive to lie. This may be because the source has no involvement with the issue, e.g. a bystander, or because their beliefs or profession require them always to be truthful.

2 **Bias** – having a motive to lie that does not come from self-interest. This may be to protect a friend, to blame someone the person doesn't like or for subconscious reasons, for example because of strongly held beliefs.

3 **Vested interest to lie** – having a motive to lie out of self-interest; this might be for self-gain or to avoid losing something, such as a job or a friend.

4 **Vested interest to tell the truth** – having a motive to tell the truth, for example because lying might endanger the source's professional reputation.

5 **Reputation** – the credibility of a source's claim is strengthened or weakened by people's knowledge of their past performance or character. However, someone's present behaviour cannot always be predicted from how they have behaved in the past.

PERCEPTION – obtaining knowledge by using the senses

6 Ability to observe – did the source really see the event?

- Eye witness provides evidence based on first-hand experience.
- Hearsay evidence is based on second-hand information.
- Character reference is evidence given about character/reputation.

7 Relevant expertise – having skills, experience or training that would help interpret the situation correctly. The evidence of an expert has more credibility than that of non-experts.

The final three criteria are particularly useful when assessing visual or documentary evidence

8 Relevance – how directly the visual or other evidence relates to the claim being made.

9 Significance – the weight of support given by the evidence when seen in the whole context.

10 Selectivity – choosing evidence to make a point, where the evidence selected may not be representative of the whole situation.

Applying the key criteria

In this chapter you will learn how to apply the key credibility criteria from Chapter 1 to:

- the overall context
- documents
- personal evidence.

You are asked to assess these areas in the first part of Unit 1 of your exam. In addition you are asked to assess the support that images give to claims; you have already covered this on pages 23–27.

Credibility of overall context

This question asks you to assess how a particular context affects the credibility of the reports that are produced, i.e. how a context would affect both documentary and personal evidence.

Types of contexts

The context chosen by the examiner is likely to be one where there is the possibility of dispute, that is, where you will eventually be answering such questions as:

- What happened?
- Who was to blame?

The contexts below are among those that could give rise to disputes:

- War – disputed reports of battle damage or outcome
- Demonstration – disputed reports of cause of damage or violence
- Sports – disputed sports results or reported actions
- Crime – disputed claims over time, place and actions
- Accident – disputed reports of cause and blame.

ACTIVITY 9

Working in pairs, look at some newspapers and pick out contexts in which there are disputes. List the contexts and keep the newspaper extracts. These will provide you with extra material for assessment when you feel ready to test out your skills.

Assessing the influence of context upon credibility

These three questions will help you to assess the possible impact of context:

1. What motives are there to misrepresent the truth?
2. What difficulties are there in perceiving the truth?
3. What difficulties are there in judging the truth?

You have seen in Chapter 1 how to use credibility criteria 1 to 7 to help you to answer the first two questions. To answer the third question you need to use the criterion of **corroboration**. When you make a judgement, if you find that two sources agree upon certain points, this is likely to be stronger evidence. However, if the context reduces the opportunity for corroboration, it might be more difficult to assess whether you should believe the report.

EXAM TIP

*Remember the first seven credibility criteria by using the mnemonic **RAVEN**:*

Reputation

Ability to observe

Vested interest (to lie or to tell the truth)

Expertise

Neutrality or Bias

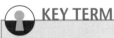

KEY TERM

Corroboration – when the evidence given by two or more sources agrees upon certain points

> *If a report about battle damage comes from a remote area of a war zone where events have happened quickly, there may be little opportunity for independent sources to be present to confirm or challenge the report. This would weaken the credibility of the report because there is little opportunity for corroboration, even though the report might be accurate.*

Corroboration is an important criterion, but it needs to be considered alongside the other criteria above when making an overall judgement. If both sources are on the same side, there may be a strong motive for them both to lie in the same way; this would weaken their evidence.

ACTIVITY 10

Make a list of ten contexts in which corroboration of evidence would be difficult, e.g. a crowded night club.

It is important to remember that you are assessing the *context in general* and not the details of any specific incident that may be reported in the documents provided. This question is intended to make you think about the difficulties associated with reporting any such event. It does not require you to refer to this *particular* incident in your answer.

Sample examination-type question

You are now going to look at how you might answer a question relating to the context of a violent demonstration.

> ## QUESTION
>
> Explain **three** ways in which the context of a violent demonstration might affect the credibility of reports that are given.

Taking each of the suggested questions from page 31 in turn, there are several possibilities that you might wish to focus upon.

1 **What motives are there to misrepresent the truth?**

There is considerable scope here to find *vested interest to lie* or distort the truth.

 **REMEMBER**

Vested interest to lie – a motive to lie, to gain or to avoid losing something

> *The media have a vested interest to misrepresent the truth if the majority of their readership sympathised with or opposed the beliefs of the demonstrators.*
>
> *The demonstrators have a vested interest to lie to claim their innocence in order to avoid prosecution, or even to lie and claim that they are guilty, in order to make themselves look good in the eyes of those supporting their cause.*

2 **What difficulties are there in perceiving the truth?**

REMEMBER

Selectivity – partial evidence e.g. choosing evidence to make a point **or** giving evidence that is partially perceived and may not be representative of the whole

> *Selectivity – In a situation where events happen quickly and in isolated pockets, it might be difficult for those giving evidence to appreciate the whole context. Their evidence might therefore be a true reflection of what was happening at that time around them, but not representative of the whole event.*
>
> *Distortion – The disorientation of fear and fast-moving events often associated with bursts of violence might also distort the perception of what actually happened.*

3   What difficulties are there in judging the truth?

> *Corroboration – If the demonstration covers a large area, there may be only one source from a particular pocket of activity; it would not be possible to corroborate or challenge the evidence given about what happened there.*

Frequently asked questions

How many points should I make?

Your questions will be presented in a booklet in which you will write your answers. This will guide you as to how many points you should make.

Can I gain marks for giving different examples?

If the question is phrased like the one on page 32, you would need to make sure that there is as little overlap between your points as possible. It is safer to make one point for each category, i.e. motive, perception and judgement, than to make two points in the same category with different applications.

If you said that there are many ways in which vested interest may affect credibility and went on to state:

> *The media have a vested interest to misrepresent the truth if the majority of their readership sympathised with or opposed the beliefs of the demonstrators.*
>
> *The demonstrators, if guilty, could have a vested interest to lie to avoid prosecution.*

you would be making two separate points about vested interest, as the applications are different.

However, you might say:

> *If the demonstrators had been guilty of grievous bodily harm they might lie to avoid a prison sentence.*
>
> *Or they might be selective in what they said and leave out important evidence so that it did not point to them.*

In this case, these two points are very closely related to the same claim about the demonstrators' vested interest. The examiner is unlikely to see them as two separate points. The safest approach would be to target each of the three areas.

 **EXAM TIP**

***Be guided by the exam booklet** as to how many points you should make.*

*Make sure that there is **no overlap between your points**.*

ACTIVITY **11**

Explain how motive, difficulties in perception and corroboration might affect the credibility of reports that are given in each of the contexts below.

A Track events at a local sports club

B Alleged thefts at a night club

C A large-scale disaster, such as an earthquake

Credibility of documents

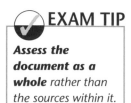

EXAM TIP

Assess the document as a whole rather than the sources within it.

This question asks you to assess the credibility of the document itself, for example a newspaper or a website. A particular author or organisation may have selected evidence from different sources or written the material themselves. It is their *choice* of sources and the *manner* in which the arguments are presented (neutrality/bias) that you will need to assess. You are not looking for weaknesses in reasoning in this part of the exam.

It is important that you treat the document as a source in itself, rather than picking out a source within it.

Suppose you are asked to assess the credibility of three documents relating to the cause of the December 2004 tsunami disaster. One of these is a scientific journal containing the conflicting reports of several experts. You would not be required to assess the experts' individual evidence at this point, but rather the credibility of the document as a whole.

You may judge it to be an unbiased report because it includes the evidence of opposing theories, that is, it has not selectively chosen the evidence of a one-sided interpretation of events. This strengthens its credibility.

Types of documents

In the exam you may be presented with written, numerical or visual material. This may be in the form of articles, reports, letters, tables of information, official minutes taken at meetings, transcripts of presentations or rules and regulations. In fact, it could be anything that might relate to the dispute presented to you. This material may be taken from sources such as newspapers, magazines, leaflets or websites.

ACTIVITY 12

Working in groups, choose a dispute that you are interested in. Collect as many different types of documents as you can that could be used as evidence. Make sure that they represent both sides of the dispute. Keep the documents to use again in Activity 13 on page 38.

The Internet is a good starting point; by using a search engine, you may find documents that provide different approaches and methods of presentation. Select a variety of formats so that you can use these later to extend your skills.

Using the key criteria to assess documents

You can use the same credibility criteria as before, but you will need to apply these in a slightly different way to documents. A document may contain several sources, so you need to assess the credibility of the sources as a group.

Neutrality

A documentary source could be said to be neutral if there is no vested interest to distort the truth or if it is impartial in what it presents. It may achieve this in one of several ways.

- By presenting a *balanced report*: providing evidence that represents both sides of the dispute rather than a one-sided account.

> An article in a scientific journal is discussing what caused the extinction of the dinosaurs. If it puts forward the case of an asteroid impact and balances this against other possible causes such as predators eating the dinosaur eggs, it is presenting more than one view – a balanced report.

- By providing *evidence that is equally representative* of each side, rather than selecting material that would show one side in a better light and disadvantage the other side.

When looking at evidence on a website it is useful to look at the URL or website address. Endings *.ac* and *.edu* indicate academic establishments, which might provide this sort of balanced evidence (see page 38).

Bias

There are several ways in which a documentary source might be seen to be biased.

REMEMBER

Bias – a motive or subconscious reason to lie or distort the truth in order to protect or blame someone else or to support strongly held beliefs

- By selecting information to support a particular belief or one side of an issue. When you are researching on the Internet, be aware that *.org* indicates an organisation. Although the material may be written by experts in the field and therefore have credibility, the way it is chosen may be biased towards the values or perspective of the organisation.

> The website of an environmental pressure group is likely to contain a number of articles against GM crops. This demonstrates their perspective. The majority of the material is against GM crops, but that is not to say that the evidence itself is not expert. The selection of the range of views is the point under assessment.

- By providing information from various perspectives but prefaced or interspersed with comments influenced by belief.
- By choosing evidence for each side selectively, to favour a particular outcome.

> *The writer of the article about the extinction of the dinosaurs might choose inexpert information about predators eating dinosaur eggs in order to discredit this position.*

Vested interest to lie

A documentary source might have a vested interest to distort the truth because its creator will benefit from the outcome. Website addresses ending *.com* and *.co.uk*, for example, indicate commercial organisations that might have a vested interest to interpret information to the advantage of their company. The ending *.gov* indicates a government source, which might also have a vested interest.

> *A government might want to put their record on employment in the best light. They could present the unemployment figures differently by reclassifying some of the unemployed as 'retraining' or 'unfit to work'. The statistics would then show falling numbers of unemployed.*

Vested interest to tell the truth

A documentary source might have a reputation of neutrality and reliability to maintain, which might strengthen the credibility of its reports.

> BBC News Online *may wish to preserve the credibility of the information they provide. Also websites ending .gov and .mil may not want to risk their credibility by straying too far from the truth.*

Assessing the credibility of websites

URL ending	Domain	Credibility?
.edu	American educational establishment	
.ac.uk	British educational establishment	
.info	Providing information	
.org	International/American organisation	
.com	International/American commercial organisation	Neutrality?
.co.uk	UK commercial organisation	Bias?
.biz	Business	Vested interest?
.net	Network company	Expertise
.gov	UK government, e.g. homeoffice.gov.uk	Reputation?
.mil	American military	
.mod.uk	British Ministry of Defence	

ACTIVITY 13

Look back at the documents you collected for Activity 12 (page 35) and use the table above to help you assess their motives or perception.

Reputation

Other documentary sources may have a reputation for sensationalism and for a very pointed bias in how they present material. This might lower the credibility of information from such sources.

Ability to observe

Where there are several sources giving evidence within one document, it is necessary to identify the proportion of eye-witness evidence and that of hearsay evidence and character reference. When the proportion of those actually at the event is significant, the credibility of the evidence is stronger than when claims are made based on past reputation or second-hand information.

> *In the case of a natural disaster a report that contained a number of eye witness reports as to the extent of the damage, might be more credible than a report that based its damage assessment on previous similar events in the area.*

Relevant expertise

You must look at the relevant expertise offered within the document, as this might be considered to be stronger than claims made at the level of the non-specialist.

> *When battle damage is reported in a war situation, the credibility of a military report would be strengthened by their expertise in perceiving the situation correctly. They would be expected to have the technical skills to identify their opponent's weapons.*
>
> *However, a newspaper report of the same situation might rely solely on the observations of civilians with limited understanding of weapons and tactics.*

Sample examination-type question

In the examination you will probably be presented with three or four documents relating to a dispute. In this discussion we will look at just one such document – this shortens the task so that you can focus on how an assessment can be made.

This document is taken from an OCR past paper belonging to the old specification. It is a fictitious report of a plane crash during a time of war between neighbouring countries. Here it is used to demonstrate how you can use these fictitious scenarios to practise the skills required by the new specification, even though the latter is likely to use text taken from real reports.

You will be asked later in this chapter to assess the evidence of the individual sources within the document, but for the moment you should focus upon the task below, which is to assess it as a document.

QUESTION

Make **two** points of assessment about the credibility of the following document. For each of these you should:

- identify the criterion of credibility that you are using
- explain how this might affect the credibility of the document
- use the text to support your answer.

The original document was not given a title or overall source. However, for the purposes of this exercise we will suppose that it is part of an article in a monthly aircraft magazine, in a dedicated section on military aircraft.

Back to the drawing board?

Has technology advanced to uncloak bombers previously invisible to radar?

In an armed conflict between neighbouring countries, a first strike bomber from Westagrum crashed onto Eastager territory. This type of aircraft was invisible to radar. There is a dispute as to the cause of the crash.

Eastager national news immediately released subtitled film footage of anti-aircraft gunners (A) in action against the Westagrum bombardment. Their jubilant voices, scarcely audible above the noise of the artillery fire, claimed, 'We tracked their plane and shot it out of the skies. They can't surprise us now. We're ready for them.'

Hours later an International Red Cross worker (R) reported that the pilots had ejected seconds before the plane hit the ground. She had treated the sole survivor for shock and exhaustion when he had escaped over the border. She added, 'They lost control after experiencing technical failure which caused the engine to stall. The plane had not been shot down.'

A video clip (V) was released some days later by the Eastager government to GNN, Global News Network. A close-up showed wreckage of the plane, identifiable by its distinctive shape, with bullet holes clearly visible in the wing. Debris of the plane was scattered along the scarred field leading to the main wreckage. An aerial shot showed the whole area cordoned off by the military, with an enclosure for international reporters who had been invited to film from a safe distance.

A press release from the Westagrum military commander (M) stated that the plane had not been attacked. It had discharged its weapons and was returning home. He claimed, 'As a developing country, Eastager does not have the advanced surveillance technology, let alone the appropriate weaponry to threaten this advanced aircraft.' He added that although these planes were noted for their high-speed manoeuvrability, the pilots had misjudged their position, pushed the agility of the plane beyond the safety limits and consequently failed to pull out of a dive. As the plane had turned, it had cart-wheeled, causing its wing to scythe through the ground.

Having recovered the aircraft's 'black box', Eastager released excerpts from the cockpit voice recorder (C). They claimed that this settled the dispute beyond any reasonable doubt, since the pilots' voices clearly admitted their defeat. Amongst recordings of the pilots losing control and making the decision to eject, they could be heard to say 'They've got us now'.

© May 2003, OCR

You can see below how to apply the credibility criteria to this document. Three points of assessment are given to illustrate how answers can be made, although only two points are required by the question above.

Motive:

> *The source, a specialist 'aircraft magazine', might have a **vested interest not to misrepresent the truth**, to protect its professional reputation in this field.*
>
> ***Neutrality** might be claimed in that it presents the dispute as a question, 'Back to the drawing board?', and includes views from both sides.*

Perception:

> *The document includes eye-witness accounts of anti-aircraft gunners and civilians together with hard evidence from a video clip and the black box: they had the **ability to observe or record** the incident at first hand.*

In each of the above answers, the criterion used to assess the credibility has been identified in bold. The text (quoted in inverted commas) has been used to support the assessment.

EXAM TIPS

- **Target** the bullet points in the question.
- **Refer** to the text to support your answer.

Frequently asked questions

How do I target the marks?

Follow the bulleted guidance on the question paper. It is likely that you will be asked for:

- a relevant criterion of credibility
- an explanation of how this applies to the document
- a reference to the text to support this.

REMEMBER

Remember to apply the first seven credibility criteria in your answer to Activity 14:

Reputation
Ability to observe
Vested interest (to lie or to tell the truth)
Expertise
Neutrality or Bias

Do I have to quote the exact words of the text?

No. You only need to use the text to support your answer, so you may simply refer to the text.

> *In the answer above regarding motive, it was only necessary to refer to the source, e.g. the aircraft magazine, to support the point that it might want to protect its professional reputation.*

In Activity 14 (page 42) you are given one document to assess, whereas in the examination you will probably be asked to assess three documents. Remember the points above as you answer this question.

ACTIVITY 14

Consider the extract below from News.Telegraph. You should make two points of assessment, for each of which you should:

- **explain what factors might have affected the credibility of the document**
- **use the text to support your answer.**

Eleven objections to the wedding of the Prince of Wales and Camilla Parker Bowles were dismissed yesterday by the Registrar General [Mr Cook]. A marriage certificate will now be granted for the ceremony at the Guildhall in Windsor next month.

The principal grounds for objection centred on whether the law allowed Prince Charles to marry in a civil ceremony. "I am satisfied that none of these objections should obstruct the issue of a [marriage] certificate," Mr Cook said.

Doubt was initially cast on whether the prince could marry in a civil ceremony because of the wording of the Marriage Act 1836, which allowed non-religious marriages to be conducted for the first time. One section said the Act should not extend to the marriage of any of the Royal Family. Most of the Act was repealed by the Marriage Act 1949, but not that particular section.

However, Downing Street, the Lord Chancellor and the four legal advisers who informed Clarence House were in no doubt of the legality of the wedding. "The Government is satisfied that it is lawful for the Prince of Wales and Mrs Parker Bowles, like anyone else, to marry by a civil ceremony in accordance with Part III of the Marriage Act 1949," the Lord Chancellor said last month.

But other lawyers, including the former Tory Attorney General Sir Nicholas Lyell, have debated the point.

Mr Cook ruled yesterday that the relevant legislation, backed more recently by the European Convention on Human Rights and the 1998 Human Rights Act, did not prevent the royal marriage. He said yesterday that in view of public interest, and with the agreement of the prince and Mrs Parker Bowles, he would issue the following statement:

"The Superintendent Registrars for Chippenham and Cirencester have received and referred to me 11 caveats objecting to the marriage of the Prince of Wales and Mrs Parker Bowles. The principal grounds of objection are that the law does not allow the Prince of Wales to marry in a civil ceremony. I have examined this matter and I am satisfied that it ought not to obstruct the issue of a certificate."

He said a reading of the 1949 Act that prevented the Prince of Wales and Mrs Parker Bowles from having a civil marriage would "interfere with their rights" under the European Convention on Human Rights.

Adapted from *News.Telegraph*, 9 March 2005

Credibility of personal evidence

Now that you have looked at how to apply the credibility criteria to the general context and to the documents as a whole, you are going to see how to assess the evidence given by personal sources within the documents.

The exam question may choose the personal sources it wants you to focus upon. They are likely to be key sources of evidence that will help you to come to a judgement about the dispute later in the paper. They are therefore likely to represent opposing sides of the dispute.

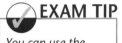 **EXAM TIP**

You can use the initials of the source to save time as long as you make it clear who you mean.

To save time, you can if you like refer to a source in your answer by using their initials, rather than writing out their name in full each time you refer to them. Write the name out in full on the first occasion you use it, putting the initials in brackets: *Justin Smith (JS) claims that ...*; after that you can use just the initials.

If the source is referred to more generally, for example by occupation, then you would use this first together with an initial: *the referee (R) ...*; this makes it clear to the examiner exactly who you are referring to.

Types of personal evidence

There are typically three types of evidence that can be offered.

- Eye-witness accounts

- Hearsay evidence

- Character reference.

You may be able to make use of these distinctions when you apply Criterion 6: *Ability to observe* to the evidence. Experience of an event at first hand can strengthen the credibility of evidence. However, you will also need to take other factors into account. The eye-witness evidence may be weakened by a vested interest to distort the truth.

> *The evidence of an invading military commander would be strengthened because he was present in the battle and experienced the events at first hand, but it would be weakened by a possible vested interest to exaggerate battle damage to increase morale.*

ACTIVITY  15

Using the documents you collected in Activity 12 (page 35), put the sources into three lists – eye-witness, hearsay and character reference.

✓ **EXAM TIP**

*Use the **bullet** **points** in the exam booklet to guide your answer.*

❗ **REMEMBER**

Suppositional reasoning – supposing something to be true in order to draw a conclusion

Using key criteria to assess personal evidence

Use the same criteria that you used to assess the credibility of documents – the first seven from Chapter 1. The question paper will state how many points of assessment it wants you to make for each person's evidence. When you make each point of assessment:

1 State the claim that you are assessing.

2 Explain how the credibility of this is strengthened or weakened by applying one of the criteria of credibility.

3 Include any factors that you must suppose to be true to reach this assessment.

> *In the case of the bystander on the edge of the public disturbance, a point of assessment relating to his evidence might read:*
>
> *The bystander's claim, 'I didn't see anyone breaking the law, only the sort of loud boisterous behaviour typical of disappointed football fans' is weakened by a vested interest to lie if they feared reprisals from those who were breaking the law.*

This assessment includes requirements 1 to 3 above.

Sample examination-type question

QUESTION

In the shoplifting scenario on page 45 consider the evidence of the shop manager and the customer.

Assess the credibility of their evidence. For each person you should make **two** points of assessment, each of which should include:

- how the claim is strengthened or weakened by any relevant factors
- any factors that you must suppose to be true to reach this assessment.

A case of shoplifting or forgetfulness?

While Laura was out shopping during the January sales for an outfit to wear at a club night out, she was accused of shoplifting. The store detective said, 'I watched her deliberately hide a pair of shoes in her bag and saw that she didn't declare them at the check out.'

Laura claimed, 'It was an honest mistake.' She added that she had chosen the shoes that she wanted to buy and had put the shoes in her bag so that she could have both hands free while she was choosing a top. She explained that by the time she got to the check out, she had forgotten that the shoes were in her bag. She said that she felt very embarrassed about the whole incident and wanted to pay for the shoes.

Laura's neighbour Amira, a shop assistant in the store, said, 'For the last couple of years the store has been short of self-service baskets during the January sales. Customers have often been forced to find other ways to carry multiple purchases.'

The store manager explained that it was not the store's policy to involve the police in all cases where customers were found in possession of store goods that they have not paid for, as some customers were genuinely forgetful. She added, 'However, we have been very pleased with our most recent store detective who has prevented the highest number of thefts within our chain of stores. I am therefore confident that this was, as he claimed, an intentional theft.'

The customer behind Laura at the checkout said, 'I felt very sorry for the lady who was apprehended by the store detective. She had complained to me about the lack of baskets when she was looking at the rail of jackets and balanced a pair of shoes on top of her bag. When she reached the checkout her arms were full. She mentioned that the time on her car parking ticket had run out whilst she was waiting in the long queue to pay for the goods. It was obvious that she forgot about the shoes.'

Below are two points of assessment for both sources, targeting the requirements of the question. You might like to go on to give further points of assessment about the other witnesses.

The customer's claim 'It was obvious that she forgot about the shoes' is strengthened by her neutrality in this situation, as she has no known motive to lie, if she was not influenced by the plight of Laura to distort the truth.

The customer's claim that Laura 'balanced a pair of shoes on top of her bag' is strengthened by the fact that the customer claimed to see this happen, if her sight was not obstructed by the other purchases that Laura had made.

The manager's claim 'I am confident that this was, as he claimed, an intentional theft' is weakened by bias if she felt that she should defend a colleague regardless of whether he was correct.

However, the same claim is strengthened by vested interest to tell the truth if making an incorrect allegation would risk her own reputation/job.

Frequently asked questions

Do I have to quote the claims?

No, but it may be easier to quote the claim than to paraphrase it. If you do put the claim into your own words you are performing an extra unnecessary task that may lead to inaccuracies and to a mistaken evaluation based on this.

If I assess the same claim twice, do I have to quote it twice?

No, you can simply say, 'The same claim is strengthened or weakened by ...'. However, where personal sources make more than one claim it is important that you make it clear to the examiner which claim you are evaluating.

 EXAM TIPS

- *If you assess the same claim twice there is no need to quote it twice.*
- *Select those claims where suppositional reasoning is more obvious.*

What should I do if there is a point of assessment that requires no suppositional reasoning?

Some points of assessment will not require assumptions to be made, and for others the assumptions are less obvious. For example:

> *The store detective's claim 'I am confident that this was, as he claimed, an intentional theft' is also weakened by the fact that it is based on hearsay evidence, as there is no reference to the manager having witnessed the event.*

Although it is a valid assessment, when it is expressed like this it shows no suppositional reasoning and any marks associated with this could not be accessed. To maximise your marks, go for those points of assessment where it is more obvious that you have to suppose something.

ACTIVITY

 EXAM TIP

Keep your answer focused upon the four elements that attract the marks.

Read the fictitious report below concerning a plane crash in a wartime situation.

Consider the evidence of the anti-aircraft gunners and the Red Cross worker and assess its credibility. For each person you should make *two* points of assessment, each of which should include:

- how the claim is strengthened or weakened by any relevant factors
- any factors that you must suppose to be true to reach this assessment.

In an armed conflict between neighbouring countries, a first strike bomber from Westagrum crashed onto Eastager territory. This type of aircraft was invisible to radar. There is a dispute as to the cause of the crash.

Eastager national news immediately released subtitled film footage of anti-aircraft gunners (A) in action against the Westagrum bombardment. Their jubilant voices, scarcely audible above the noise of the artillery fire, claimed, 'We tracked their plane and shot it out of the skies. They can't surprise us now. We're ready for them.'

Hours later an International Red Cross worker (R) reported that the pilots had ejected seconds before the plane hit the ground. She had treated the sole survivor for shock and exhaustion when he had escaped over the border. She added, 'They lost control after experiencing technical failure which caused the engine to stall. The plane had not been shot down.'

A video clip (V) was released some days later by the Eastager government to GNN, Global News Network. A close-up showed wreckage of the plane, identifiable by its distinctive shape, with bullet holes clearly visible in the wing. Debris of the plane was scattered along the scarred field leading to the main wreckage. An aerial shot showed the whole area cordoned off by the military, with an enclosure for international reporters who had been invited to film from a safe distance.

A press release from the Westagrum military commander (M) stated that the plane had not been attacked. It had discharged its weapons and was returning home. He claimed, 'As a developing country, Eastager does not have the advanced surveillance technology, let alone the appropriate weaponry to threaten this advanced aircraft.' He added that although these planes were noted for their high speed manoeuvrability, the pilots had misjudged their position, pushed the agility of the plane beyond the safety limits and consequently failed to pull out of a dive. As the plane had turned, it had cart-wheeled, causing its wing to scythe through the ground.

Having recovered the aircraft's 'black box', Eastager released excerpts from the cockpit voice recorder (C). They claimed that this settled the dispute beyond any reasonable doubt, since the pilots' voices clearly admitted their defeat. Amongst recordings of the pilots losing control and making the decision to eject, they could be heard to say, 'They've got us now.'

Background information

- **Aircraft invisible to radar** *are used as first strike bombers to take out a nation's surveillance and communications infrastructure, so that second strike bombers are less vulnerable.*
- **The International Red Cross** *is a charity which provides healthcare and aid in times of war, disaster and need.*
- **An aircraft's 'black box'** *records conversations in the cockpit, and information about how the aircraft's systems are functioning. It is designed to be indestructible in the event of an impact. Its recordings are used to help determine the cause of a crash.*

© OCR, May 2003

Is there anything else that I will be asked in relation to personal evidence?

You may be asked separate questions regarding the strength of the claims, with reference to their reasoning.

Sometimes sources do not make direct claims, but use *inference*. Others make claims that require *assumptions* to be made or use *flawed reasoning*. Some may use *principle* or *analogy* to strengthen their reasoning.

SUMMARY

CONTEXT

- Ask the following questions to assess the possible impact of the general context upon the credibility of the claims:

  1 What **motives** are there to misrepresent the truth?

  2 What difficulties are there in **perceiving** the truth?

  3 What difficulties are there in **judging** the truth?

- Assess the **context in general** and not this specific dispute.

DOCUMENTS

- Assess the **whole** document rather than the separate sources within it.
- Assess credibility using **RAVEN**.
- Do not look for weaknesses in reasoning.
- Look at any **website addresses**, as an indication of the likely credibility of the document.
- Target your answer to the **exact bullet points** in the exam question.
- Refer to the **text** using quotes to avoid possible inaccuracies when using your own words.

PERSONAL EVIDENCE

- If you prefer, you can use **the initials** of the sources to save you time, but remember to make clear what the initials stand for in the first instance.
- Target your answer to the **exact bullet points** in the exam question.
- Keep the reference to the text **brief** and **focused** on what you are assessing.
- Select those claims where **suppositional reasoning is more obvious**.

Producing a reasoned judgement

 **KEY TERM**

Judgement – a
conclusion reached
after weighing up
the likelihood of
which side is more
credible

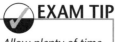 **EXAM TIP**

*Allow plenty of time
for this section of the
paper.*

 **EXAM TIP**

*Target your answer
directly to what the
question asks you to
do.*

Now you are going to practise the skills that will to help you to answer the final question on the paper, *'Come to a reasoned judgement as to how likely it was …'*. To do this you need to assess which side of the dispute has the greater credibility of evidence.

This section is likely to represent a third of the paper. The question may appear to be shorter, but you need to allow plenty of time for your answer. The task requires you to make a judgement, bearing in mind the assessments that you have made previously. Bringing this information together takes time.

Making a reasoned judgement

A reasoned judgement can be made in several different ways. However, the question will give you guidance that will allow you to target the marks available.

The exam question is likely to include the elements that are shown in bold in the question below. This chapter will use this question and the shoplifting scenario to show you how to come to a judgement by considering *corroboration and conflict*, *balance of evidence*, *weight of evidence* and *quality of evidence*.

Sample examination-type question

> Come to a reasoned **judgement** as to how likely it was that Laura intentionally stole the shoes.
>
> You should include the following in your answer, which should refer to the individual sources:
>
> - three precise points of **corroboration** and **conflict** – support these with reference to the text
> - a discussion of the **balance** of evidence
> - an explanation of the **weight** of evidence
> - an assessment of the **quality** of evidence.

A case of shoplifting or forgetfulness?

While Laura was out shopping during the January sales for an outfit to wear at a club night out, she was accused of shoplifting. The store detective said, 'I watched her deliberately hide a pair of shoes in her bag and saw that she didn't declare them at the check out.'

Laura claimed, 'It was an honest mistake.' She added that she had chosen the shoes that she wanted to buy and had put the shoes in her bag so that she could have both hands free while she was choosing a top. She explained that by the time she got to the check out, she had forgotten that the shoes were in her bag. She said that she felt very embarrassed about the whole incident and wanted to pay for the shoes.

Laura's neighbour Amira, a shop assistant in the store, said, 'For the last couple of years the store has been short of self-service baskets during the January sales. Customers have often been forced to find other ways to carry multiple purchases.'

The store manager explained that it was not the store's policy to involve the police in all cases where customers were found in possession of store goods that they have not paid for, as some customers were genuinely forgetful. She added, 'However, we have been very pleased with our most recent store detective who has prevented the highest number of thefts within our chain of stores. I am therefore confident that this was, as he claimed, an intentional theft.'

The customer behind Laura at the check out said, 'I felt very sorry for the lady who was apprehended by the store detective. She had complained to me about the lack of baskets when she was looking at the rail of jackets and balanced a pair of shoes on top of her bag. When she reached the check out her arms were full. She mentioned that the time on her car parking ticket had run out whilst she was waiting in the long queue to pay for the goods. It was obvious that she forgot about the shoes.'

Now you will look at how, taking each of the requirements of the question in turn, you can build up the skills necessary to make a reasoned judgement:

1　Judgement
2　Corroboration and conflict
3　Balance of evidence
4　Weight of evidence
5　Quality of evidence.

1 Judgement

To make a judgement you will need to assess which side of the dispute has the greater credibility of evidence. Your judgement will be the conclusion you draw from bringing together your assessments of the evidence provided.

In the disputes presented to you the decision may be difficult to make, but there are no right or wrong judgements, only relevant ones. Provided you focus on the question to make a relevant

EXAM TIPS

- *Don't spend time agonising over which judgement to make.*
- *Make sure your judgement is supported by your assessment.*
- *Make sure your judgement relates directly to the question.*

judgement, it does not matter which side of the dispute you support. Your judgement must be supported by your responses to the other elements of this question.

In this scenario the choice is either that a theft took place, or that Laura had a moment of forgetfulness. Either judgement would gain a mark provided that your assessment in the rest of the question supported it.

At this stage the answer could be:

> *It is more likely that Laura had not intentionally stolen the shoes because of the following …*

You should make sure that your judgement relates directly to the question. Here the question asks you to judge whether a theft did take place. If you answered, 'It is more likely that the store was to blame because there were not enough baskets', this would not be a direct response to the question, since the judgement should focus upon Laura's intention.

You do not need to come to a judgement at the beginning of this question. You can use the tasks set in the question to help you to draw this conclusion at the end. Considering corroboration and conflict, together with the balance, weight and quality of evidence, may help you to resolve any indecision regarding your judgement.

2 Corroboration and conflict

 **REMEMBER**

Corroboration – where the evidence given by two or more sources agrees upon certain points

Focusing upon the key issue, in this case either a theft or forgetfulness, you will be looking at the claims made by the sources and identifying where they agree and disagree.

The question might ask you for three points of corroboration and three points where the sources have conflicting claims. One point for each will be developed here as an example of what is required.

Corroboration

Corroboration requires you to identify what is agreed upon by two or more sources.

- It is not sufficient to simply identify the two sources that agree.
- You should be looking for a point that directly relates to the judgement that you are making.
- It should not be a minor detail that would have no consequence for the judgement.

In this case the answer could be:

> *Both Laura and the customer claim that the shoes were not intentionally stolen.*

However, if you were to give the answer: 'Both Amira and the customer refer to the lack of self-service baskets', you would *not* be identifying corroboration that directly relates to the judgement.

You are then asked to support your answer from the text. You are not required to use quotes, but it may be easier to do so. If you paraphrase the claims you are performing an extra task, and by putting the claims into your own words you risk making mistakes, such as changing the meaning or leaving out essential qualifying words.

In this case the claims to support the point of corroboration are:

> *Laura claimed that 'It was an honest mistake' … that when she went to the check out, she had forgotten that the shoes were in her bag.*
>
> *The customer claimed, 'It was obvious that she forgot about the shoes.'*

Conflict

Conflict requires you to identify where two or more sources give conflicting evidence. You might expect to find conflict between sources who are on opposing sides of the dispute, but sometimes sources who support each other differ in the details of what they claim, and this has a bearing on the judgement.

In this case the answer could be:

> *Laura and the store detective's evidence conflicts as to whether this was an intentional theft.*
>
> *Laura claimed, 'It was an honest mistake', while the store detective claimed, 'I saw her deliberately hide a pair of shoes in her bag and not declare them at the check out.'*

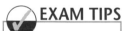

EXAM TIPS

- *Corroboration and conflict should relate directly to the judgement.*
- *Using quotes to support these points may be easier and safer than paraphrasing.*
- *Make sure your judgement is supported by your assessment.*
- *Make sure your judgement follows directly from the question.*

ACTIVITY 17

Consider the shoplifting scenario again and identify a further point of corroboration and of conflict. Support your answers from the text. Use the exam tips on the left to help focus your answers.

3 Balance of evidence

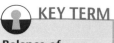
KEY TERM

Balance of evidence – an explanation of which source supports which side of the dispute

When you were identifying points of corroboration and conflict, you may have become clearer about which sources supported each other on each side of the dispute. This will form the basis of identifying the **balance of evidence**, which requires you to explain which sources support each other. In the example here:

> • *The manager supports the store detective, while the customer supports Laura.*
>
> • *Amira could be taken to support Laura but does not comment directly on the incident.*

EXAM TIPS

• *Make sure you include all the sources.*

• *Explain about those that do not easily fit on either side.*

This explanation could be made clear by *additionally* expressing it in a diagram:

> *Manager and Store detective*   v   *Laura and Customer*
> *Amira*

As the exam question is likely to involve a greater number of sources, you will need to make sure that you include all the sources in the balance of evidence.

Identifying the balance also requires you to explain about *problem sources*, i.e. those that do not fit easily on either side:

- where a source does not directly support one side of the dispute, but their claims *could* be used to do so, like Amira in the case above

- where sources make several claims, some of which support one side and others which could be taken to support the other side, i.e. they support *both* sides

- where sources are *neutral*, i.e. they give contextual information that does not support either side.

ACTIVITY 18

Look back at Activity 14 on page 42. Identify the balance of evidence in the article relating to the legality of a royal marriage in a civil ceremony.

KEY TERM

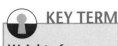

Weight of evidence – a numerical assessment of which side has the greater number of sources supporting it

4 Weight of evidence

The **weight of evidence** is a numerical assessment drawn from the balance of evidence. You have to give the number of sources on each side, and state which side has the greater number. You could present this information in the form of a ratio.

> *Either of the following interpretations could count as good answers:*
>
> *In this case, the weight of the evidence could be argued to be equally balanced, with two sources supporting each side, i.e. a ratio of 2:2, if Amira's evidence is not seen as giving support to Laura.*
>
> *However, it could equally be argued that the weight of the evidence is on the side of Laura 3:2, if Amira's evidence is argued to give indirect support to Laura.*

The weight of evidence is just one of the factors in deciding the strength of evidence. It is often argued that the fact that there are more sources supporting one side in a dispute should sway our decision. However, another factor to be taken into consideration is whether the weight of sources provides credible evidence – *quality of evidence* must also be taken into account.

5 Quality of evidence

KEY TERM

Quality of evidence – an assessment of the overall credibility of all the evidence given for each side of the dispute

The significance of the strength of numbers on one side, however, may be weakened if the **quality of the evidence** that they give is weak.

To assess quality of evidence you need to apply the credibility criteria to assess the overall credibility of each side of the dispute. Asking these three questions will help you to determine where the strengths lie on each side of the dispute:

1 Does one side have less motive to lie?

2 Did one side have more opportunity to observe the event at first hand and without restrictions?

3 Does one side have more relevant expertise to be able to interpret the events correctly?

It may be that the better quality of evidence lies not with the weight of sources, but with the side that has fewer claims to support it.

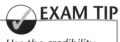

- You will probably be asked to look for three points of comparison, as in the example below.

> *There is a stronger element of vested interest to lie on the side of the manager and store detective to protect their jobs and the store,*　V　*whereas on Laura's side, neither Amira nor the customer have a vested interest to lie.*
>
> *The support for the store detective's evidence depends upon the character reference of the manager, who is not said to have been present at the event,*　V　*whereas Laura's evidence is supported by the account of an eye witness, the customer.*
>
> *The experience of the store detective, the most recent store detective, may be less than that of Amira.*　V　*Amira, commenting on the lack of baskets over the past couple of years, may have more experience than the store detective and therefore be able to judge the context with more insight.*

- Make sure that you make clear which side has more quality of evidence. You could do this as you make the comparisons, or sum up the points after the comparisons, as follows:

> *Therefore on the side of Laura there appears to be less of a motive to lie for gain, more ability to observe the event, and if Amira is included, arguably more experience and insight.*

From the above it might therefore be argued that the quality of evidence supporting Laura's claim (that she did not intentionally steal the shoes) is stronger than that of evidence given by the opposing side. This assessment would support the initial judgement made on page 52, which means that the judgement mark could also be gained.

Look back over the exam tips in this chapter and use them to help focus your answers in Activity 19.

In this activity the familiar scenario of the plane crash has been extended to include more sources of personal evidence. This provides you with the opportunity to practise the skills required, but the question has been scaled down to help you to focus on the individual tasks. It differs from the exam paper question in that it offers only one documentary source. It also requires only one point of corroboration and one point of conflict.

ACTIVITY

! REMEMBER

- Focus upon the question.
- Target the exact point of corroboration.

✓ EXAM TIPS

- *Make clear the difference between direct claims and evidence that is provided.*
- *If there are not enough points of direct corroboration you may need to look for points that could corroborate if assumptions are made.*

Read the information on page 58 and come to a reasoned judgement as to how likely it was that the plane was shot down. You should include the following in your answer, which should refer to the individual sources:

- one precise point of both corroboration and conflict – support these with reference to the text

- a discussion of the balance of evidence

- an explanation of the weight of evidence

- an assessment of the quality of evidence.

In an armed conflict between neighbouring countries, a first strike bomber from Westagrum crashed onto Eastager territory. This type of aircraft was invisible to radar. There is a dispute as to the cause of the crash.

Eastager national news immediately released subtitled film footage of anti-aircraft gunners (A) in action against the Westagrum bombardment. Their jubilant voices, scarcely audible above the noise of the artillery fire, claimed, 'We tracked their plane and shot it out of the skies. They can't surprise us now. We're ready for them.'

Hours later an International Red Cross worker (R) reported that the pilots had ejected seconds before the plane hit the ground. She had treated the sole survivor for shock and exhaustion when he had escaped over the border. She added, 'They lost control after experiencing technical failure which caused the engine to stall. The plane had not been shot down.'

A video clip was released some days later by the Eastager government to GNN, Global News Network. A close-up showed wreckage of the plane, identifiable by its distinctive shape, with bullet holes clearly visible in the wing. Debris of the plane was scattered along the scarred field leading to the main wreckage. An aerial shot showed the whole area cordoned off by the military, with an enclosure for international reporters who had been invited to film from a safe distance.

A press release from the Westagrum military commander (M) stated that the plane had not been attacked. It had discharged its weapons and was returning home. He claimed, 'As a developing country, Eastager does not have the advanced surveillance technology, let alone the appropriate weaponry to threaten this advanced aircraft.' He added that, although these planes were noted for their high-speed manoeuvrability, the pilots had misjudged their position, pushed the agility of the plane beyond the safety limits and consequently failed to pull out of a dive. As the plane had turned, it had cart-wheeled, causing its wing to scythe through the ground.

Having recovered the aircraft's 'black box', Eastager released excerpts from the cockpit voice recorder (C). They claimed that this settled the dispute beyond any reasonable doubt, since the pilots' voices clearly admitted their defeat. Amongst recordings of the pilots losing control and making the decision to eject, they could be heard to say, 'They've got us now.'

© OCR, May 2003

Additional sources

1 An international news report published details of the rescue of the pilot. It claimed that helicopters used global navigation systems and advanced radar technology to avoid detection, track the pilot and pick him up just as he had crossed the border. His rescuers claimed, 'He was in good shape.'

2 Civilians from Eastager claimed, 'We saw the bomber and anti-aircraft artillery being fired in its direction, from which a ball of fire fell from the skies. The plane crashed into a field only yards from where we were crouching at the edge of woodland taking cover from the bombardment.'

SUMMARY

- Allow plenty of time for this section.
- Target your answer directly to what the question asks you to do.

JUDGEMENT

- Make sure that your judgement relates directly to the question.
- Make sure that your judgement is supported by your assessment.

CORROBORATION AND CONFLICT

- Choose points that are directly related to the judgement.
- Quote directly from the text to support your points; this avoids possible inaccuracy in putting the claim into your own words.
- Be precise: only quote the parts of the claim that actually agree or conflict.
- If points of direct conflict are few, look for lack of agreement.

BALANCE OF EVIDENCE

- Include all the sources, including non-personal ones, for example photographs.
- Explain those that do not easily fit on either side.

WEIGHT OF EVIDENCE

- Comment on how you are using the problematic sources.

QUALITY OF EVIDENCE

- Use all ten credibility criteria to focus your comparison.

Preparing for the exam

Before the exam

The work you have done in this book, and the examination-type questions you have worked through, should have helped to develop the skills and understanding to approach the questions. In your exam preparation, make sure that you:

- know and understand the ten credibility criteria
- can apply them to different kinds of evidence
- understand how to come to a reasoned judgement.

Your teacher may be able to provide you with past papers to practise on.

Critical Thinking is about just that – thinking logically. You don't have to learn lots of facts to show the examiner what you know. However, you do need to be able to think clearly in the exam. Finish your preparation in good time, try to get a good night's sleep and allow plenty of time to get to the exam – arriving late and flustered is a bad start.

In the exam

Dividing up your time

EXAM TIPS

Allow approximately:

- *15 minutes to read the documents and questions*
- *20 minutes for each area.*

You are advised to spend up to 15 minutes reading the documents and questions.

This will leave you 60 minutes to write out your answers and gain a possible 80 marks. If you look at the mark breakdown of the paper, you will see that there are three areas tested that have roughly equal marks. Giving these areas equal time means that you will have 20 minutes each to:

- assess the credibility of documents
- assess the credibility of personal evidence
- come to a reasoned judgement.

Reading the documents and questions

If you read through the questions and *identify what judgement you are being asked to make* in the last question, you might have a clearer idea of what the passages are about. You can then read through the documents and work towards this when you assess the evidence.

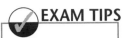 **EXAM TIPS**

It is a good idea to find the two sources that you are asked to assess in the question on personal evidence and annotate their evidence using the credibility criteria to help you later.

You might find it useful to identify each separate source and highlight them with colours to show which side of the dispute they support. This will help you later when you write about balance and weight of evidence.

What will the examination paper look like?

The questions asked on the exam paper will differ from year to year. They will depend upon the type of dispute chosen and the nature of the documents you are given to assess. However, there are some things you can safely expect.

- You are likely to be given three or four documents of about two A4 pages in total.
- These could relate to a dispute in one of many areas. It could be a historical, scientific, environmental, medical, social, legal or artistic dispute.
- You will be asked to:
  - assess the credibility of documents
  - assess the credibility of personal evidence
  - come to a reasoned judgement.

Knowing how much to write

 **EXAM TIP**

You will have an answer booklet in the examination in which to write your answers. In this there will be prompts and numbers to guide some of your answers.

- The space left between the prompts can act as a guide to how much you should write.
- The marks for each answer or part answer can also act as a guide. For example, if only one mark is allocated, you would not be expected to write as much as a paragraph.
- In general, you can write using bullet points or continuous writing.

However, the important thing is not the length of your answer, but how good it is. Some people write very succinctly, making their points quickly and directly. Other answers get there in the end, but include much that is irrelevant or unfocused.

Five marks are available for the 'quality of written communication'. The examiner will be looking for writing that is well organised and in an appropriate style using specialist vocabulary, with accurate spelling, grammar and punctuation.

Guidance to the activities

ACTIVITY 1

Work in a group. You might expect the following sources, under normal circumstances, to be unbiased. Think of as many reasons as you can why each of the sources might not be neutral when making claims.

There are many reasons why the neutrality of each of the following might be weakened. Here are some examples for you to consider. You might like to add to this list.

A A religious leader

A religious leader might be expected to be neutral *because they may feel bound by such religious beliefs as 'thou shalt not bear false witness' which direct them to tell the truth,*

but this neutrality would be weakened if there was a higher ranking value that conflicted with this, for example, preventing the loss of life. Thus, in circumstances where giving correct information might lead to innocent people being killed, a religious leader might feel justified in not giving that information.

B A competition judge

A judge deciding who is best in a competition might be expected to be neutral *and to make an objective judgement as otherwise this might endanger her reputation for professional competence,*

but this neutrality would be weakened if she felt that she should judge one particular event in such a way that it produced a fair balance of results overall. For example, she might positively discriminate to ensure a gender, age or ethnic balance in the results.

C A football referee

A football referee might be expected to be neutral *and to give an objective judgement because he is trained to treat the performance of each side equally,*

but this neutrality would be weakened if he was so annoyed by insults from the supporters of one of the teams that he favoured their opponents.

D A health and safety inspector

Health and safety inspectors might be expected to be neutral because they are trained to identify risky or illegal practice using specific criteria,

but this neutrality would be weakened if they revisited a workplace where they had faced opposition to their inspection previously, and had become prejudiced against the workers there.

E The BBC news

The BBC news would be expected to be neutral because it has a reputation of neutrality in its reporting of events, and it would be in its interest not to be seen to distort the truth by presenting the news selectively,

but this neutrality would be weakened if it decided were in the national interest to present the truth selectively, for example in wartime or during a national emergency such as an epidemic, in order to keep national morale high.

In each case additional circumstances have been identified which, if true, could enable you to draw a conclusion that would question the neutrality of these sources and therefore the strength of the credibility of their claims.

ACTIVITY ❷

In the shoplifting scenario identify which sources could be said to be biased and which to have a vested interest. Justify your decisions by giving reasons.

- *Laura's claim that 'it was an honest mistake' would be weakened by a **vested interest to lie about her intentions** in order to avoid prosecution if she was guilty of shoplifting.*

This is different from biased evidence, as her motive to lie would be influenced by self-interest – avoiding a negative outcome for herself.

- *Amira's claim 'the store is sometimes short of self-service baskets' would be strengthened if motivated by a **vested interest to tell the truth** to retain her job.*
  *However, we would need to balance this against the possibility of her claim being weakened by **bias** if she felt the need to help her neighbour, motivating her to exaggerate the problem of the lack of self-service baskets.*

Here both vested interest (self-interest in her job) and bias (to support her neighbour) are involved.

- *It could be argued that the store detective's claim that Laura was 'deliberately hiding a pair of shoes' may be weakened by a **vested interest** to be productive **if** his job involved a minimum quota of results and he was driven to identify as many shoplifters as possible. This might make him overzealous in claiming that a deliberate theft had taken place, instead of pointing out that the shoes had not been paid for, allowing for the possibility of a genuine forgetful moment.*

Here self-interest – to demonstrate vigilance – may have prompted an exaggerated claim.

ACTIVITY 3

Working in groups, examine a variety of newspaper articles. List the claims that are based on an appreciation of reputation, whether positive or negative.

Newspaper articles may seek to give credibility to present actions on the basis of past good practice. Suppose that a politician with a reputation for honesty and fair practice in his political life was accused of using his position to help a friend. His claims of innocence would be given credibility by his reputation, and most people would give him the benefit of the doubt. However, his past behaviour does not necessarily mean that he behaved correctly in this case.

ACTIVITY 4

Differentiate between eye-witness or primary evidence, hearsay evidence and character reference in the source in Activity 2.

In each case:
- **hearsay** should be something heard secondhand
- **character reference** should refer to past experience and not this event.

Some examples:

Primary evidence	Hearsay evidence	Character reference
Laura: 'It was an honest mistake.'	The checkout operator: 'I heard the person behind Laura in the queue say that Laura had complained to her about the lack of baskets when she was looking at tops.'	The checkout packer: 'I have known Laura since we started school together and she has always been very honest.'

ACTIVITY ❺

Work in a group to identify restrictions to observation. Outline a scenario and give the claims of one or more sources where there is restricted sight and one or more where there is restricted hearing.

Responses could develop any of the restrictions discussed, for example, observing an incident while:

- facing south on a sunny day (restriction of vision)
- at a venue where everyone was joining in with the music (restriction of hearing)
- travelling in the next lane of traffic (restriction of vision).

An example of a weakened case might be:

- a bouncer's claim that he heard one of those accused of starting a fight in a busy night club shout out, 'Get that lot!', might be weakened if the music and audience participation was so loud that it would be difficult to pick out what anyone was saying.

ACTIVITY ❻

In each of the examples below, differentiate between relevant and irrelevant expertise.

a) **State the expertise of the source.**
b) **Identify the expertise required to make the claim.**
c) **Decide whether the source's expertise is relevant in this case.**
d) **Justify your decision.**

A The athlete would have expertise in his field of sport, but this would not necessarily be relevant to the nutritional expertise required to recommend a specific food as being healthy. Thus their particular expertise would not strengthen the credibility of their claims. Their own fitness may be the result of a combination of many other factors apart from eating this particular food.

B The UK weather reporters or the people who advised them would have the relevant expertise in weather forecasting to assess the severity of impending weather to make such advice credible, though not certain.

C Jamie Oliver would have relevant expertise as a chef to make his contribution to a debate about nutrition and diet credible. However, this is a reported comment and not the expert's own words, so the advantage of expert comment has to be balanced against the possibility of sensationalism and exaggeration to attract viewers, although in this case it was an accurate reflection.

ACTIVITY 7

One great dispute about the beginning of the universe is whether or not it was caused by a Big Bang. What relevance would this image have to the dispute?

*This image could be assessed as a diagram to **explain** the connection of events in the Big Bang theory. As no claims are made, its relevance to the dispute is difficult to assess.*

ACTIVITY 8

Look at the leaflet below. Assess what support the photograph gives to the claims that are made.

First identify the claims:

- 'The needs of the local community are not being addressed'
- 'The present congested road network is seriously affecting both local business and the quality of life of the townsfolk.'

Next assess the support that the photograph gives to the claims. The photograph shows a stream of cars approaching a set of traffic lights in a town centre. The degree to which this illustrates a town centre congestion problem depends upon its relevance, selectivity and significance, as follows:

Relevance

- *The claim is about the present congested road network, whereas the photograph is of a congested town centre road. The terms of reference are different, although the latter is obviously part of the overall context.*

- *The title refers to the community's needs not being addressed. A photograph taken at one specific moment cannot take into account the previous condition of the roads. This might be an improvement upon previous conditions. It also does not take into account what plans there may be to address these needs.*

- *In addition, the claim is that local business and quality of life are being affected. The photograph simply illustrates a queue of traffic and not the effects that this causes.*

Selectivity

- *If the traffic conditions on this road were not representative of those elsewhere in the town centre **or** if this road had been selected because its congestion was the worst in the town, then the image could be claimed to have been selectively chosen to lend support to an exaggerated claim.*

Significance

With regard to the conditions in the photograph, the significance of the queue would depend upon the context of the photograph:

- *If this represents a queue at traffic lights where only a few cars move through at a time rather than a queue that quickly disperses once the lights changed…*

- *If this represents the beginning of a much longer queue rather than the end of a short queue…*

- *If this represents traffic at all times of the day at this point rather than or a short period during a peak time…*

… then the image would give greater circumstantial support to the claim that congestion was affecting business and the quality of life.

ACTIVITY 9

Working in pairs, look at some newspapers and pick out contexts in which there are disputes. List the contexts and keep the newspaper extracts. These will provide you with extra material for assessment when you feel ready to test out your skills.

Choose the contexts that interest you most. If you have a range of newspapers you might be able to collect several articles on the same dispute, but with different sources within them. You could use this later to develop the range of your assessment skills.

If you do not have many newspapers at hand you could try using the Internet – choose a topic that interests you and enter this into the search engine.

ACTIVITY 10

Make a list of ten contexts in which corroboration of evidence would be difficult.

Your answers could include:

- *accidents at sea*
- *mountaineering incidents*
- *satellite failure*
- *incidents in remote parts of the Third World with little technology*
- *incidents where people work alone.*

ACTIVITY 11

Explain how motive, difficulties in perception and corroboration might affect the credibility of reports that are given in each of the contexts below. Use the exam tips to help focus your answers

Three effects have been identified for each context to illustrate the types of answers that could be given. You will see that it is not necessary to write a paragraph for each point made. Keeping your answer focused will save you time.

A Track events at a local sports club

- **What motives could there be to misrepresent the truth?**

There might be a vested interest by competitors, coaches or club members to distort the truth to influence results or to provoke disqualifications in favour of their own team.

- **What difficulties might there be in perceiving the truth?**

Unless the event were being recorded, it might be difficult for those making decisions to see exactly what happened in a split second from their particular angle of view over a large track.

- **What difficulties might there be in judging the truth?**

There might be difficulties in resolving conflicting interpretations as there might be few neutral spectators.

B Alleged thefts in night clubs

- **What motives could there be to misrepresent the truth?**

The night-club owners might have a vested interest to distort the truth because they want to protect their trade by bringing about a prosecution that could act as a future deterrent.

- **What difficulties might there be in perceiving the truth?**

If the incident took place in a crowded room where everyone's attention was focused on the entertainment and their powers of perception were blunted by alcohol, no one might notice the theft or be able to remember exactly what happened.

- **What difficulties might there be in judging the truth?**

If only a few people notice the theft and most people are influenced by the effects of alcohol, there might be little opportunity for precise corroborating claims.

C A large-scale disaster, such as an earthquake

- **What motives could there be to misrepresent the truth?**

Newspapers might have a vested interest in selecting the worst hit areas in order to produce a more gripping front page that would attract more buyers.

- **What difficulties might there be in perceiving the truth?**

Some of the damage might be in areas that have become inaccessible because of the disaster, so that it is difficult to perceive the overall damage accurately.

- **What difficulties might there be in judging the truth?**

It might be difficult to corroborate reports from remote or very inaccessible areas.

ACTIVITY 12

Working in groups, choose a dispute that you are interested in. Collect as many different types of document as you can that could be used as evidence. Make sure that they represent both sides of the dispute.

Guidance was given within the activity. You can use the documents you collect here for Activities 13 and 15.

ACTIVITY 13

Look back at the documents you collected for Activity 12 and use the table above to help you assess their motives or perception.

This activity gave you practice in using the information about websites in the table. Interpreting web addresses might give you possible assessment points in the examination.

ACTIVITY 14

Consider the extract from *News.Telegraph*. You should make *two* points of assessment, for each of which you should:
- **explain what factors might have affected the credibility of the document**
- **use the text to support your answer.**

Motive

- *Although the document centres largely on the decisions of the Registrar General, Mr Cook, other sources on both sides of the debate are mentioned:*

  '... Downing Street, the Lord Chancellor and the four legal advisers who informed Clarence House were in no doubt of the legality of the wedding'

  '... other lawyers, including the former Tory Attorney General Sir Nicholas Lyell, have debated the point.'

  This gives a thinly balanced account which might be considered as unbiased. However, it could be argued that by presenting the argument of Mr Cook unchallenged the document is biased.

- *The Daily Telegraph is a broadsheet newspaper with a reputation to maintain. It may therefore have a vested interest not to distort the truth so that it maintains this reputation and its readership.*

Perception

- *The document includes the views of experts in this field. For example, it might be expected that the Registrar General would have the necessary expertise to give a valid decision regarding whether legislation prevented the royal marriage in a registry office.*

You will notice from the above answers that a reference to the text is all that is required. In some instances it may only be a reference to the names of the sources.

ACTIVITY **15**

Using the documents you collected in Activity 12, put the sources into three lists – eye-witness, hearsay and character reference.

It might be interesting to discuss your findings with other groups to find out what was the most usual percentage of eye-witness evidence used and whether this depended more on the type of dispute or on the type of document.

ACTIVITY **16**

Read the fictitious report on page 47 concerning a plane crash in a wartime situation.

Consider the evidence of the anti-aircraft gunners and the Red Cross worker and assess its credibility. For each person you should make *two* points of assessment, each of which should include:

- **how the claim is strengthened or weakened by any relevant factors**
- **any factors that you must suppose to be true to reach this assessment.**

- *The anti-aircraft gunner's claim 'We tracked their plane and shot it out of the skies' is weakened by their vested interest to lie if the plane had crashed and they wanted to boost their national morale by claiming to have dealt with the advanced technology of their opponents.*

- *The same claim is strengthened by their ability to observe the plane being hit by gunfire as they were targeting overhead planes, if the bombardment was not so heavy that there was confusion about which planes were hit and whether their gunfire actually brought them down.*

- *The Red Cross worker was not an eye-witness, so her claim 'The plane had not been shot down' is weakened by the fact that she did not actually see the event, so the credibility of her report depends upon the claims of the pilot. He might have a vested interest to lie about the event if he wanted to maintain the integrity of his nation's aircraft as being imperceptible to radar.*

In this claim, the explanation is a little longer because it involves looking into the motives of the source of the Red Cross worker's information.

- *The same claim is strengthened by the source's neutrality as a Red Cross worker with an impartial aid role, if this reflects an impartial stance and she has not been influenced by the plight of the pilot.*

ACTIVITY 17

Consider the shoplifting scenario again and identify a further point of corroboration and of conflict. Support your answers from the text. Use the exam tips on page 53 to help focus your answers.

Corroboration

Both the store detective and the manager claim that an intentional theft had taken place:

- *The store detective claims, 'I saw her deliberately hide a pair of shoes in her bag and not declare them at the check out.'*
- *The manager claims, 'I am therefore confident that this was, as he [the store detective] claimed, an intentional theft.'*

In the first example of corroboration, we looked at how Laura and the customer corroborate in their evidence, to support the judgement that Laura did not intentionally steal the shoes. This answer directly relates to the other side of the dispute in the judgement that you are asked to make.

Conflict

The evidence of the manager and the customer conflicts as to whether there was an intentional theft.

- *The manager claims, 'I am therefore confident that this was, as he claimed, an intentional theft.'*
- *However, the customer claims, 'It was obvious that she forgot about the shoes.'*

In the first example of conflicting evidence, we looked at the main characters in the dispute, Laura and the store detective. Here the conflict is between sources who give supporting evidence to each of these.

ACTIVITY 18

Look back at Activity 14 on page 42. Identify the balance of evidence in the article relating to the legality of a royal marriage in a civil ceremony.

- *The only person actually giving evidence is the Registrar General.*
- *Support is claimed from Downing Street, the Lord Chancellor and four legal advisors from Clarence House.*

ূ

- *There is an assertion that the issue has been debated by others - the former Tory Attorney General and lawyers - but no details of the challenge are given.*

This record of the balance of evidence demonstrates the type of report that has been made. It is not a balanced account of a dispute, but rather information being given within a known context of views on either side.

This illustrates that if you want to collect information to assess a fully represented dispute, you may need to look for more than one document so that you have more viewpoints expressed. On the other hand, you may find a single document that explicitly includes the views of both sides in the dispute. For a single document that more adequately performs this function.

ACTIVITY 19

Come to a reasoned judgement as to how likely it was that the plane was shot down. You should include the following in your answer, which should refer to the individual sources:

- one precise point of both corroboration and conflict – support these with reference to the text
- a discussion of the balance of evidence
- an explanation of the weight of evidence
- an assessment of the quality of evidence.

Corroboration

First consider this answer:

Both the anti-aircraft gunners and the video clip give evidence that the plane had been shot down.

The anti-aircraft gunners claim: 'We tracked their plane and shot it out of the skies'.

It is claimed that the video clip shows evidence of: 'the wreckage of the plane identifiable by its distinctive shape with bullet holes clearly visible in the wing'.

This answer focuses directly upon the question and is very precise in its support from the text. It is brief, but sufficient. It correctly makes clear where:

- sources have made direct claims

- claims are made from hard evidence (note that the video itself does not make claims, it can only provide evidence of events).

Now consider this second possible answer:

Both the civilian witnesses and the black box give evidence that the plane was shot down.

The civilian witness claims: 'We saw the bomber and anti-aircraft artillery being fired in its direction, from which a ball of fire fell from the skies.'

The black box provides evidence that the pilots said: 'They've got us now.'

This answer goes further than the claims being given, since neither example is direct evidence of the first-strike bomber being shot down.

To make this claim about the civilian witness's evidence, you would have to assume that the artillery fire hit the plane and brought it down. However, the plane might have had engine failure which caused its descent, and the artillery fire might have caught it as it was already in the process of crashing down.

You would also have to interpret the pilot's words as meaning that they had been shot, rather than that they had engine failure and were about to crash into enemy territory. If you had to use this point for corroboration you would need to state the suppositional reasoning that would be necessary to make the claim that the plane was shot down: *That is only if the artillery fire hit the plane and brought it down.*

Now consider this third possible answer:

Both the Red Cross worker and the international news report claim that the pilot survived.

The Red Cross worker reports that she had 'treated the sole survivor for shock ….'

The international news reports that the rescuers claim, 'He was in good shape.'

Although a correct point of corroboration, this answer is not relevant to the judgement that needs to be made about whether the plane was shot down.

Conflict

First consider this answer:

The evidence of the Red Cross worker and of the anti-aircraft gunners does not agree about what happened to the plane.

The Red Cross worker claims: 'The plane had not been shot down.'

The anti-aircraft gunners claim: 'We tracked their plane and shot it out of the skies.'

This answer is focused and fully related to the question asked.

Now consider this alternative answer:

The international news report and the Red Cross worker's evidence conflict about the condition of the pilot.

The international news reports that the rescuers claim: 'He was in good shape.'

The Red Cross worker reports that she had: 'treated the sole survivor for shock ...'.

There are two problems with this answer.

- It does *not* focus upon the judgement about the plane. The pilot's condition is irrelevant to this.

- Although the reports do not claim the same thing, they *do not necessarily conflict.* The pilot may have been in good shape, that is without physical injury, but have been exhausted and in a state of shock.

Balance of evidence

The video clip and the civilians both support the anti-aircraft gunners that the plane was shot down, whilst the Westagrum military commander and the Red Cross worker both claim that it was not shot down.

Other sources are more problematic:

- *The black box evidence could be used to support either side depending upon how it is interpreted.*

- *The international news report is not relevant to the judgement.*

EXAM TIP

Make sure that you include all the sources in the weight, including those that are inconclusive or irrelevant.

This answer could be additionally expressed for clarification as:

Video clip, civilians, anti-aircraft gunners	V	Military commander, Red Cross worker

Black box evidence

International news report irrelevant.

You would need to explain your comment about the civilians and the video clip. Just because the civilians saw the weapons launched and the plane crash does not mean that the weapons hit the plane, and the video clip recording of the wreckage does not confirm a weapon strike without further information.

Weight of evidence

The weight of the evidence is on the side that the plane was shot down, 3:2. Three sources support this claim, whereas two sources could be used to challenge it. One source is inconclusive and a further is irrelevant to the judgement.

This answer accounts for all the sources, even though two cannot be directly included in the judgement.

Quality of evidence

There is a balance of neutrality and vested interest on both sides.

*Two sources (civilians and anti-aircraft gunners) have a **vested interest to lie** but their claims are supported by the **hard evidence** of the video clip and the black box if a particular interpretation is made.*

*The military commander has a **vested interest to lie** to protect the reputation of the aircraft as invisible, but the Red Cross worker is a **possible independent source** supporting this claim, if the pilot's claim were true.*

There are more eye-witness sources on the side claiming the plane was shot down:

*The anti-aircraft gunners and the civilians are **eye witnesses**, together with **the hard evidence** of the video clip and the black box,*

*whereas both the military commander's and the Red Cross worker's evidence depends upon **second-hand information.***

There may be more of a vested interest to tell the truth on the side that the plane was shot down:

The release of the video clip to GNN might mean that the video evidence was reliable, if the **reputation** *of an independent news network were involved,*

whereas the military commander's **reputation** *might present less of an incentive to tell the truth, if balanced against his motive to protect national morale.*

The quality of the evidence would appear to be slightly in favour of the plane being shot down, given that there is an independent source supporting this, and hard evidence that could be seen as corroborating the claim.

However, you need to realise that in this practice activity, only one documentary source was used. This has limited the range of the assessment. If there had been more documents, other perspectives might have been present to give a more evenly balanced number of sources on the two sides.

Judgement

It is more likely that the aircraft was shot down.

This claim is supported by the assessment of the quality of the evidence above.

Glossary

Ability to observe – the ability of a source to use any of their senses to asssess the event

Assumption – what must be supposed to be the case to draw your conclusion

Balance of evidence – an explanation of which source supports which side of the dispute

Bias – a motive or subconscious reason to lie or distort the truth in order to protect or blame someone else or to support strongly held beliefs

Character reference – evidence given about the character or reputation of one of the sources involved, which doesn't relate to the event itself

Conclusive evidence – evidence that leaves little room for doubt

Context – the situation in which the evidence arises, e.g. a football match

Corroboration – when the evidence given by two or more sources agrees upon certain points

Credibility – whether the evidence is believable

Credibility criteria – tools to help you assess whether a claim is believable

Dispute – situation where the evidence is inconclusive, that is, incomplete, unclear or open to interpretation

Documentary evidence – any evidence of a textual nature, such as newspaper articles and websites

Eye witness – someone who provides evidence based on first-hand experience

Hearsay evidence – evidence based on second-hand information from another source, who may have interpreted it

Hypothetical reasoning – see **Suppositional reasoning**

Judgement – a conclusion reached after weighing up the likelihood of which side is more credible

Motive – reason to lie or to tell the truth

Neutral – having no motive to lie

Perception – obtaining information by using the senses

Personal evidence – a claim made by a witness or other contributor

Quality of evidence – an assessment of the overall credibility of all the evidence given for each side of the dispute

Relevance – how directly the evidence relates to the claims being made

Relevant expertise – the skills, experience or training that would help a person interpret the situation correctly

Reputation – when knowledge of past performance or of character is used to strengthen or weaken the credibility of present claims

Selectivity – choosing evidence to make a point

Significance – the weight of support given by the evidence when seen in the whole context

Source – where the evidence comes from; it could be a person or a document

Suppositional reasoning – supposing something to be true to draw a conclusion; also known as **hypothetical reasoning**

Vested interest – a motive to lie or to tell the truth because the person has something to gain or to avoid losing

Visual evidence – any evidence of a non-textual nature, such as photographs, maps, tables and line drawings

Weight of evidence – a numerical assessment of which side has the greater number of sources supporting it

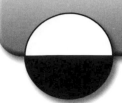

Index